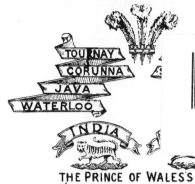

THE PRINCE OF WALES'S OWN
(WEST YORKSHIRE REGIMENT)

EXTRACT FROM DIGEST OF SERVICE

OF THE

2ND BATTALION

THE PRINCE OF WALES'S OWN

(WEST YORKSHIRE REGT.)

IN SOUTH AFRICA

FROM OCTOBER 20th, 1899, TO AUGUST 4th,
1902.

The Naval & Military Press Ltd

in association with

The National Army Museum, London

Published jointly by

The Naval & Military Press Ltd
Unit 10 Ridgewood Industrial Park,
Uckfield, East Sussex,
TN22 5QE England

Tel: +44 (0) 1825 749494
Fax: +44 (0) 1825 765701

www.naval-military-press.com
www.military-genealogy.com
www.militarymaproom.com

and

The National Army Museum, London
www.national-army-museum.ac.uk

Printed and bound in Great Britain by
CPI Antony Rowe, Chippenham and Eastbourne

*In reprinting in facsimile from the original, any imperfections are inevitably reproduced
and the quality may fall short of modern type and cartographic standards.*

EXTRACT FROM DIGEST OF SERVICE OF
THE 2ND BATTALION THE PRINCE OF
WALES'S OWN (WEST YORKSHIRE REGT.)
IN SOUTH AFRICA, FROM OCTOBER 20TH,
1899, TO AUGUST 4TH, 1902.

The Battalion, strength as under,

> 27 Officers,
> 1 Warrant Officer,
> 935 Non-Commissioned Officers and Men,

embarked at Southampton in ss. "Roslin Castle" on October 20th, 1899, for conveyance to South Africa, to form part of the 2nd Brigade, 1st Division.

2nd Brigade, under the command of General Hildyard, C.B., consisted as follows:—

> 2nd Queen's.
> 2nd Devonshire.
> 2nd West Yorkshire.
> 2nd East Surrey.

October 25th.—Arrived at Las Palmas about 5 a.m., after a calm and uneventful voyage. Sailed again at 6 p.m. Received here the news of the Glencoe and Dundee fights.

November 8th.—Arrived Capetown about 10 p.m., after a calm voyage. One death occurred on voyage:—No. 4616 Pte. W. Wiffin, who died on the 8th and was buried at sea on the 9th inst.

November 9th.—Orders received for the Brigade to proceed with all haste to Natal, owing to the Natal Field Force being besieged in Ladysmith. Sailed at 11-30 a.m.

November 11th.—Arrived at Durban, and anchored off the bar about 11 p.m.

1

November 12th.—Proceeded into harbour at 9 a.m. and disembarked. The following Officers landed in South Africa with the Battalion :—

Colonel F. W. Kitchener, Commanding.
Major H. de C. Hobbs, 2nd in command.
    „   W. Fry.
    „   C. J. M. Heigham.
    „   J. C. Yale.
Captain T. Berney.
    „   C. J. Ryall.
    „   W. S. Carey.
    „   J. S. Bartrum.
    „   A. C. Daly, Adjutant.
Lieut. L. H. Spry.
    „   S. G. Francis.
    „   G. L. Crossman.
    „   O. H. L. Nicholson.
    „   A. M. Boyall.
2nd Lieut. M. G. Cantor.
    „   C. C. Bicknell.
    „   A. H. Cuthell.
    „   M. B. B. Riall.
    „   F. J. Lemon.
    „   A. M. Ross.
    „   J. C. Gretton.
    „   C. A. Cooke.
    „   E. A. Porch.
    „   C. J. H. Lyster.

Sergeant-Major, subsequently promoted Qr.-Master, C. Richards. Attached, Lieut. H. S. Pennell, V.C., Derbyshire Regiment.

The Battalion went in three trains to Maritzburg, arriving from 5 to 7 p.m. ; detrained and proceeded to Rest Camp. 2nd Lieut. C. A. Cooke and 37 N.C.O.'s and Men detailed for duty at the base (Maritzburg).

November 13th.—At 2 a.m. the Battalion entrained and proceeded to Estcourt, arriving about 10 a.m. The Garrison at Estcourt consisted of 2nd Dublin Fusiliers, 1st Border Regt., Durban Light Infantry, 2 Guns Natal Volunteer Artillery, small detachment of Imperial Light Horse and Natal Carbineers, the whole under the command of Colonel C. Long, R.H.A. The position was considered critical, as the Boers were reported advancing from Colenso.

November 14th.—At 10 a.m. the Boers reported in sight, advancing to Hodgson's Farm, about four miles north-west. Garrison assembled under arms and outposts reinforced. Boers, after reconnoitring position from Hodgson's Farm, retired. Heavy rain fell all night, causing great discomfort as Camp had been struck.

November 15th.—About 7 a.m. rapid artillery fire was heard from north-east of position, lasting a few minutes. This proved to be an engagement between armoured train and Boers. The armoured train and 1 Naval 7-pounder were captured.

The escort was provided by the Dublin Fusiliers under the command of Captain Haldane, Gordon Highlanders.

November 16th.—Garrison reinforced by 2nd Queen's, 2nd East Surrey, and 2 Batteries R.F.A.

The outposts sentries at this time were very severe, it being no uncommon thing for Companies to be 48 hours on duty, as more than half the Garrison were required for the picquet line.

November 17th.—A, B, D, E, and H Companies under command of Colonel Kitchener marched to Willow Grange (distance eight miles), with orders to reinforce detachments K.R.R.M.I., Natal Carbineers, and Imperial Light Horse.

November 18th.—At Willow Grange.

November 19th.—At Willow Grange. Boers reported moving round south from Weenen towards Highlands, which is south of Willow Grange.

November 20th.—Returned to Estcourt. Whilst at Willow Grange outposts were very heavy, 4 out of 5 Companies being continuously on duty.

November 21st.—Very severe thunderstorm. 2 Naval 12-pounders under command of Lieutenant James, H.M.S. "Tartar," arrived at 6 p.m. D, F, G, and C Companies marched out in the direction of Willow Grange to cover retirement of flying Column (all arms) which was returning to Estcourt.

November 22nd.—Information received that a strong force of Boers had reached Willow Grange and were holding a position at Highlands. At 2-30 p.m. a Force consisting of 2nd West Yorkshires, 7 Companies of East Surreys, 4 Companies of 2nd Queen's, 1 12-pounder Naval Gun, and 7th Battery R.F.A., under command of Colonel Kitchener, proceeded in the direction of Willow Grange and occupied Beacon Hill, about seven miles south of Estcourt and overlooking the Valley of Willow Grange. The hill was occupied about 5 p.m. without resistance, the Boers firing three or four shots from a Creusot Gun, situated on the Highlands, at the Troops as they crested Beacon Hill, and were replied to by the Naval Gun. Just as the hill was occupied a terrific thunderstorm came on which re-occurred at intervals until about 1 a.m. The afternoon had been intensely hot and sultry, consequently the men had their lightest clothes on, but the night was intensely cold, every one being drenched to the skin. The ½ Battalion West Yorkshire Regiment, which Major Hobbs commanded, was sent forward under cover of the storm on to one of the spurs of Beacon Hill overlooking the Highlands position. The other ½ Battalion West Yorkshire Regiment, under Major Fry, and the East Surreys were ordered to join them. Keeping under cover of the enemy, this was accomplished with great difficulty owing to the roughness of the ground and the intense darkness. The remainder of the Force bivouacked under shelter west of Beacon Hill. About midnight the West Yorkshires and East Surreys were ordered to advance and assault Bryn-bella Hill at dawn, and to capture a Creusot Gun which was in position there. The advance was led by Guide Mr. Chapman, and for a considerable distance, owing to the steep and rocky ground, had to be conducted in single file, West Yorkshires leading; eventually more ground was reached and West Yorkshires and East Surreys were formed in parallel columns. Shortly before reaching the foot of Bryn-bella Hill through some regretable error some of the East Surreys opened fire on the West Yorkshires; several shots were fired, but luckily order was quickly restored; unfortunately, Drummer Russell was killed and two men of the East Surreys. The advance was then resumed, and we shortly reached the point from where the attack was to be delivered. From this point a wall led straight up the hill into the enemy's position. The West Yorkshires were formed on the right of the wall, and the East Surreys on the left. The advance was made by double Companies, the leading double Companies led by Major Hobbs. At 2-50 a.m. the assault was delivered. As the first line approached the summit a Boer sentry challenged and promptly opened fire, the leading line doubled to the front, the sentry was bayoneted, and the hill taken, one other Boer being bayoneted, one taken prisoner, and about 30 horses captured; subsequently it was found that their big gun had been moved at 2-30 a.m., the Boers being apprehensive of an attack. The further crest of the hill was promptly occupied just as dawn was breaking: one could then see parties of Boers moving upon Highland Hill and occupying trenches, shortly after opening fire on our men, who had had no time to erect any cover. Arrangements had been made for the remainder of the Force to co-operate with us at dawn, but owing to some error this did not take place; for about one and a-half hours the Boers kept up an ineffective fire on our position, only one man being hit. The Boers then brought up a Vickers-Maxim at about 1,800 yards range, and very quickly found our range, and after that their musketry fire became very effective; they also opened fire with a Creusot Gun from a hill to the south of Highlands at very long range. The position under this fire quickly became untenable, especially as the supply of ammunition was running short, and the order to retire was given. Just as the retirement commenced some of the Imperial Light Horse and Natal Carbineers under Colonel Marby came up and were of much assistance, helping the retirement. Just as we had retired off the hill the Queen's, Border Regiment, and Battery arrived too late. The retirement was continued to Estcourt, which was reached about 6 p.m.; our losses were 11 killed.

KILLED.

No. 5198 Lce.-Corpl. Whitely, H.
„ 5136 Pte. Benson, J.
„ 2966 Drummer Russell, H.
„ 2616 Pte. Dickson, A.
„ 2587 Pte. Rudd, A.
„ 3099 Pte. Gibbs, M.
„ 2294 Pte. Newton, J.
„ 5129 Pte. Thornton, J.
„ 2435 Pte. Smith, J.
„ 2250 Pte. Morgan, W.
„ 5116 Pte. Tobin, S.

2nd Lieut. Ross and 49 Men wounded, 2 subsequently dying of their wounds. The Guide Chapman was found on return to Camp to have been killed.

November 24th.—Quiet day in Camp. Ambulance and white flag went out to fetch in wounded, who had been well treated by Boers. Lce.-Corpl. Whitely and Drummer Russell were buried.

November 25th.—All quiet. Our Guide, Mr. Chapman, whose sad fate has been already mentioned, was buried, and the movement started to get up a subscription in the Regiment for a Memorial in Estcourt Church. Ptes. Dixon and Gibbs died of wounds.

November 26th.—Bearer Coy. proceeded to battlefield to bury the dead. It was subsequently ascertained that the Boer losses in the engagement were 30 killed and 100 wounded. At 8 a.m. the whole Force paraded and marched to Frere (distance about 11 miles), which was reached about 7 p.m., after an intensely hot and trying march, the men suffering much from want of water. This movement was decided on as it was ascertained that the Boers had retired on Colenso, fearing for their Communications.

November 27th.—Frere. Camped alongside Howell's Farm, Mr. Howell kindly placing his Farm at our disposal as an Officers' Mess.
Men occupied in entrenching outposts' position. A few shots fired by 7th Battery R.F.A. at a small party of Boers, who promptly dispersed.

November 28th.—Occupied in entrenching position.

November 29th.—Entrenching as usual. 2 4·7 Naval Guns arrived.

November 30th.—2nd Devonshire Regt. arrived, making the Brigade complete.

December 1st.—Captain Mansel-Jones and 2nd Lieuts. Barlow and Grant-Dalton joined.

December 2nd.—Battalion paraded at 9 a.m. and practised the attack near William's Kopje. Naval 12-pounder fired a few shots at a looting party of Boers.

December 3rd.—Sunday service at 8-15 a.m. in Queen's Camp. A reconnaissance of Mounted Troops, 5 Companies Queen's, 1 Border Regiment and 2 Naval 12-pounders. Started at midnight towards Chieveley.

December 4th.—At 4 a.m. Battalion marched out to outposts' line in the direction of Chieveley, to support reconnaissance, which returned at 5-30 a.m., and we returned to Camp. At 9 a.m. practised the attack in front of No. 8 Picquet.

Congratulatory order issued by General Buller, expressing his approval of the conduct of the Regiment at the action near Willow Grange.

December 5th.—Nothing to note.

December 6th.—Ditto.

December 7th.—Ditto.

December 8th.—Practised attack in the morning, moved Camp in the afternoon.

December 8th.—General Lyttelton's Brigade arrived in Camp.

December 9th.—Fusilier Brigade arrived.

December 10th.—Nothing worthy of note.

December 11th.—Battalion paraded in the morning. Semaphone Signalling practised.

Fusilier Brigade marched to Chieveley. Heat intense.

December 12th.—Inspected by C.O. in the morning.

December 13th.—Nothing to note.

December 14th.—Struck Camp at 2-30 a.m. and marched to Chieveley, about 7 miles. Naval guns bombarded Colenso in the afternoon.

December 15th.—Struck Camp, laagered wagons at 2-30 a.m. and advanced to the Battle of Colenso, 2nd Brigade forming centre column, Devons and Queen's in firing line, East Surreys 2nd line, and the West Yorkshires in reserve. The day was intensely hot, the Battle lasting from about 6-30 a.m. to about 2 p.m., when the retirement was commenced.

2nd Lieut. Ross wounded.

ORDERS issued by General Buller on the morning of December 15th, 1899.

1.—The enemy is entrenched in the kopjes north of Colenso Bridge. One Camp is reported to be near the Ladysmith Road, about five miles north-west of Colenso; another Camp is reported in the hills which lie north of the Tugela, in a northerly direction from Hlangwaini Hill.

2.—It is the intention of the G.O.C. to force the passage of the Tugela to-day.

3.—The 5th Brigade will move off at 4-30 a.m. and cross at the Bridge Drift immediately west of the junction of Doornkop Spruit and the Tugela, and, after crossing, will move down the left bank of the river towards kopjes north of iron bridge (*i.e.*, road bridge).

4.—The 4th Brigade will advance at 4-30 a.m. to a point between Bridle Drift and the railway, so that it can support either 5th or 2nd Brigade.

5.—The 6th Brigade, less ½ Battalion escort to baggage, will move at 4 a.m. to a position whence it can protect right flank of 2nd Brigade, and, if necessary, support it, or the Mounted Troops, referred to later on, moving towards Hlangwaini Hill.

6.—The O.C. Mounted Troops will move off at 4 a.m. with a force of 1,000 Men and 1 Battery of No. 1 Brigade Division in the direction of Hlangwaini Hill to cover the right flank, and take up a position on Hlangwaini Hill, whence he can enfilade the kopjes north of iron bridge; forces of 300 and 500 Cavalry will also watch the right and left flanks respectively.

7.—The 2nd Brigade Division R.F.A. will follow the 4th Brigade, and take up a position whence it can enfilade the kopjes north of iron bridge. 6 Naval Guns, 2 4·7 and 4 12-pounders, will come into action on right of 2nd Brigade Division.

R.F.A. (less 1 Battery detached with Mounted Brigade) will proceed under cover of 6th Brigade to a place whence it can prepare the crossing of the 2nd Brigade; the other 6 Naval Guns will act with this Brigade Division.

8.—The 2nd Brigade will move from its present camping ground at 4 a.m., and, passing south of present camping ground of No. 1 and 2 Divisional Troops, will move to a point between the railway line and the Artillery west of railway, whence it can secure these Guns and await their preparatory fire before advancing to cross the Tugela at Colenso with the object of gaining the kopjes north of iron bridge.

BRIGADE ORDERS by General Hildyard, C.B.

The 2nd Brigade will be formed as follows:—

(a) 1st Line—2nd Queen's on right, 2nd Devons on left, with a Battalion front of 400 yards.

2nd Line—At a distance of about 800 yards ½ Battalion West Yorkshire Regt., with Head Quarters on the right, 2nd East Surrey Regt. on the left.

3rd Line—½ Battalion West Yorkshire Regt. (at the immediate disposal of the Major-General) will follow at about 800 yards.

(b) The first objective will be the village of Colenso. After this has been occupied, the 2nd Queen's will endeavour to effect a passage at the railway bridge; and the 2nd Devons at the iron road bridge and at the drift which is reported to be 50 yards west of it up-stream.

(c) Should only one passage be gained, the 2nd Line will be pushed through at that spot and assist in seizing the kopjes, the Battalion at the other passage assisting the operation with its fire, and eventually forming fresh reserve.

(d) Should a passage be effected at both points, connection will be re-established as soon as possible between the Battalion.

10.—The O.C. R.E. will detail a detachment with explosives and wire nippers to accompany each Battalion in 1st Line. He will arrange to reconnoitre passages as possession of the bank is gained, and will endeavour to establish a means of crossing at the most favourable spot.

11.—The ambulances of the Bearer Company will follow the 3rd Line, the dressing station will be established as far forward as practicable on the railway in a sheltered position.
The O.C. Bearer Company will make his own arrangements for the collecting station immediately in rear of the troops.

12.—The O.C. 2nd West Yorks. Regt. will keep two of the orderlies of the 1st Royal Dragoons with him in the 2nd Line; the remainder are to march with the 3rd Line.

13.—The ammunition mules and S.A.A. carts, from which the ammunition is expended before crossing the river is to be replaced, will accompany the Battalions. The remainder will form the Brigade ammunition reserve, in rear of 3rd Line (an Officer, 2nd West Yorks. Regt.).

14.—Each Infantry Soldier will carry 150 rounds on his person, the ammunition now being carried in the ox wagons of regimental transport being distributed.

15.—Great coats will not be carried but will be placed in two ox wagons of regimental transport.

16.—As soon as the Troops mentioned in the preceding paragraphs have moved to their positions, the remaining Units and the baggage will be formed in deep formation facing north. Five separate Lines under Qr.-Masters in rear of to-day's Artillery position, the right of each Line resting on railway, but leaving a space of a 100 between railway and right flank of line. In 1st Line, counting fr. m the right, Ammunition Column, No. 1 Divnl. Troops, 6th Brigade Field Hospital, 4th Brigade Field Hospital, Pontoon Troops R.E., 5th Brigade Field Hospital, Ammunition Column. No. 2 Divnl. Troops in 2nd Line, counting from the right, baggage, 6th Brigade, 4th Brigade, 5th Brigade, and 2nd Brigade.

4th and 5th Lines, counting from right, Supply Columns in same order as baggage in 2nd and 3rd Lines.

Lieut.-Col. Reeves will command these details.

G.O.C. 2nd Brigade will be with the 3rd Line.

Battalion arrived at Camp about 5 p.m. after a trying day, during which the Troops behaved with the utmost gallantry.

December 16th.—Armistice for 24 hours to bury dead. Our casualities—2nd Lieut. Ross, wounded by a fragment of shell, in leg.

December 17th.—Struck Camp at 2-30 a m. and retired about two miles towards Chieveley Station.

December 18th.—Naval Guns bombarded enemy's position and destroyed road bridge.

December 19th.—Camp routine. Daily bombardment by Naval Guns. One or two small Cavalry patrol affairs.

December 20th.—Ditto   ditto

December 21st.—As on December 19th and 20th.

December 22nd.—Ditto   ditto

December 23rd.—March to Blaaukraanz River and bathed near monument erected in memory of massacre of Boers by Zulus.

December 24th.—Sunday Church parade and usual bombardment.

December 25th.—Christmas Day. Sports held in afternoon.

December 26th.—Officers' Race Meeting. Captain Berney won the open Mile on his famous grey, " Yorkshire Tom."

December 27th.—Camp routine and usual bombardment.

December 28th.—Ditto   ditto.

December 29th.—Ditto   ditto.

December 30th.—Ditto   ditto.

December 31st.—Ditto   ditto.

1900.

January 1st.—Camp routine and usual bombardment.

January 2nd.—Ditto   ditto.

January 3rd.—Ditto   ditto.

January 4th.—Ditto   ditto.

January 5th.—Ditto   ditto.

January 6th.—At 3 a.m. very heavy firing heard, big guns and even musketry, in direction of Ladysmith, which continued all day. About 11 a.m. heliograph received from Ladysmith, via

Umkulinbo: - Boers attacked in force at 2-45 a.m., repulsed with loss on all sides; Lord Ava dangerously wounded in head.

At 1-30 p.m. assembly sounded and Force turned out for demonstration in front of Colenso. Guns shelling the Boer position, the Boers did not reply.

January 7th.—Camp routine and heavy rain.

January 8th.— Ditto   ditto.

January 9th.—Ditto   ditto.

January 10th.—Struck Camp at 4 a.m. and Force ordered to march to Pretorius' Farm, about eight miles west of Chieveley. Battalion on rear-guard had hard work, as Naval 12-pounders had to be constantly man-handled over drifts and soft ground. After taking about five hours to march four miles Battalion was ordered to make detour by Zietmann's Farm with Naval Guns so as to get on better roads. Remainder of Force proceeded direct to destination.

Halted at Zietmann's Farm for two hours to outspan oxen and feed. Arrived in Camp about 6 p.m. at Pretorius' Farm— a fine one, evidently one of the original settlers in the country : fine trees and a good orchard.

January 11th.—Paraded at 4 a.m. and made demonstration towards river by Deal Drift; a few Boers seen on opposite bank of river. Thorneycroft's M.I. reconnoitred to river bank, but Infantry and Guns did not get within range. On return to Camp about mid-day heard that Cavalry Brigade under Lord Dundonald had seized Potgieter's Drift, 4th Brigade pushed on to hold it. Warren's Division camped at Springfield, Hart's Brigade about two miles west of us.

January 12th.—Force remained in Camp.

January 13th.—Force remained in Camp. Outpost Companies report Boers trekking in westerly direction from Deal Drift.

January 14th.—Sunday, remained in Camp.

January 15th.—3 a.m., struck Camp; marched to Springfield, about 12 miles; Battalion formed Advanced Guard, baggage late in Camp as it had to make a long detour to cross Little Tugela by Springfield Bridge.

January 16th.—At 4-40 p.m. marched on right. Scale of baggage, Officers, 20 lbs. each, Men's great coats, and one day's ration, 3 wagons in all. Joined Warren's Force under Mount Alice, marched under cover of darkness about nine miles in direction of Trichard's Drift, arrived on heights above drift about 1 p.m., and bivouacked at dawn. D and H Companies were ordered at dawn to reconnoitre drift, and reported all clear.

Force then marched to drift, and Royal Engineers started to make pontoon bridge and were fired at by a few Boers, one man of Devons being killed. They were, however, driven off by a few long range volleys from H Company. Guns then shelled a farm on the other side of the river and the neighbouring heights, but there were no Boers there. B, D, E, and F Companies under command of Major Fry were ferried across the river in pontoons and occupied position to cover construction of bridge, which was completed during the afternoon.

The Lancashire Brigade relieved ½ Battalion in the evening, whereon the latter took up comfortable quarters in the farm.

January 18th.—Baggage and guns and remainder of Force crossed, remainder of Battalion crossed at dusk, and the Battalion bivouacked one mile north of the Tugela.

January 19th.—Marched to Venter's Drift, Battalion forming the Advanced Guard. On arrival at drift Battalion was ordered to make a road over drift and crossing shoulder of hill on opposite side; this was done in one and a-quarter hours. Battalion much complimented by R.E.'s on their work.

After breakfast, Force advanced about two miles further in direction of Acton Holmes, halting during day, whilst Cavalry reconnoitred in direction of Acton Holmes; in the evening re-crossed drift and bivouacked by side of spruit.

January 20th.—Lancashire Brigade and Hart's Brigade advanced against enemy's position on heights west of Spion Kop.

Towards the afternoon they had gained the near end of ridge. At 5 p.m. West Yorkshires moved up in support of Hart's Brigade, prolonging the line to the left; this was accomplished in the dark, cold, and wet night.

January 21st.—Firing resumed at daybreak, lasted all day. An advance towards enemy's position was attempted but found to be perfectly impossible as it was an absolutely open Glacis leading up to their entrenchments. In some Companies as many as 300 rounds per man were fired, and the M.G. fired 7,500 rounds during the day.

CASUALTIES.

KILLED.

Officer.

Capt. Ryall.

Men.

No. 3917 Pte. Buckle, D.
,, 3404 Pte. Owen, J.
,, 5010 Pte. Crozier, G.
,, 2679 Pte. Kershaw, E.
,, 5364 Pte. Gascoigne, W.

2nd. Lieut. Barlow and 42 Men wounded. Casualties chiefly amongst G Company under Captain Ryall, and one section of E Company under Lieut. Boyall, which made gallant attempts to rush enemy's entrenchments.

January 22nd.—Firing continued all day. About mid-day Battalion retired to Venters Spruit to protect baggage and left rear of Force. Captain Ryall buried at Fairview Farm.

January 23rd.—Firing still continued all day. At 1-30 p.m. Battalion proceeded to Sugar Loaf Hill and relieved 2nd Devons. Entrenched ourselves, firing heavy till nightfall, but no casualties.

January 24th.—Sangars were built all previous night, and firing continued all the day, but owing to good cover only one man wounded.

January 25th.—Same position; still a heavy fire; Lancashire Brigade stormed Spion Kop, dominating position on enemy's left: during the day they were subjected to heavy shell firing, and during the night withdrew after suffering heavy loss.

January 26th.—Still in same position; still a heavy fire. About mid-day A, B, E, and G Companies, under command of Major Fry, were withdrawn to a position about one mile in rear, to be ready if necessary to cover retirement. At 8 p.m., a general retirement of the whole Force was carried out under great difficulties owing to heavy rain and thick mist. At dusk precautions had been taken to mark line of retirement by placing Men at 25 yards' interval, which enormously facilitated matters. The march continued all night, and at dawn the following day the whole of the Troops had re-crossed the Tugela by the pontoon bridge; Men were much exhausted, but coffee was made, and rum issued, and Men marched cheerily into Camp about four miles further on.

January 27th.—Tents arrived from Spearman's Farm about 5-30 p.m.

January 28th.—Sunday. Rested in Camp.

January 29th.—Moved Camp to Spearman's Hollow, about one and a-half miles south-east.

January 30th.—Major Watts, Captain Tew, and 2nd Lieut. Fryer, with draft of 177 N.C.O.'s and Men, joined from England. 2nd Lieut. Ross joined us again from Hospital.

January 31st.—Nothing worthy of note.

February 1st.—Remained in Camp.

February 2nd.—Ditto.

February 3rd.—General Warren's Division moved from Springfield to Potgieter's.

February 4th.—Camp struck after Church Parade, and Battalion marched to neck of Mount Alice, near Potgieter's, and bivouacked for the night.

February 5th.—At daybreak marched to plain north of Zwartz Kop. General Wynne's Brigade and Field Artillery made a feint attack towards Brakfontein. About 10 a.m. Guns were retired by successive Batteries under very long range fire, crossed the

Tugela to south by pontoons and opened fire on Vaal Krantz, the real point of attack. After a heavy bombardment, in which Naval Guns from Mount Alice and Zwartz Kop and Howitzers from the plain joined, Lyttelton's Brigade crossed to north bank of Tugela by pontoon bridge and attacked and captured Vaal Krantz by its southern shoulder.

The 2nd Devons crossed the Tugela in support, when all further movements were suspended owing to darkness, and the Force bivouacked on south side of Tugela.

February 6th.—At dawn Boers opened fire on bivouac with a Long Tom from Doorn Kop and made accurate shooting but did little damage.

The day spent in trying to master enemy's artillery fire by our Howitzers and heavy guns. At dusk 2nd Brigade ordered to relieve Lyttelton's Brigade on Vaal Krantz Hill, which was completed about 8 p.m.; night spent in building sangars under an occasional sniping fire from the Boers.

February 7th.—At dawn, and from then, the hill was subjected to a very heavy shell and Pom-pom fire from front and both flanks; no losses suffered, however, owing to excellent cover. A continuous rifle fire was kept up throughout the day. The firing line consisted of A Company under Major Yale, D Company under Captain Mansel-Jones, 1 Section E Company under Lieutenant Boyall, and F Company under Major Watts. At 9 p.m. the Brigade was withdrawn, and re-crossed the Tugela, bivouacking in front of Zwartz Kop. Casualties—2nd Lieutenant Bicknell and four Men slightly wounded, a few Men being bruised by stones dislodged by shells. The other Regiments of the Brigade suffered considerable loss.

February 8th.—At 4 a.m. the Force marched to Springfield.

February 9th.—Remained in Camp.

February 10th.—At 5 a.m. marched to Pretorius' Farm.

February 11th.—At 3 a.m. marched to Chieveley, and pitched Camp near Blaaukrantz River.

February 12th.—Remained in Camp.

February 13th.—Remained in Camp, and received news that Lord Roberts had entered Free State.

February 14th.—At 6 a.m. Force marched to Hussar Hill. Artillery and Cavalry were engaged with Boers at Hlangwaini; bivouacked for the night.

February 15th.—Marched to Moord Kraal. Country very hilly and covered with thick scrub. Artillery engaged.

February 16th.—Remained in bivouac. Guns bombarded enemy's position on Green Hill. 2nd and 4th Brigades carried out reconnaissance.

February 17th.—At 6 a.m. 2nd Brigade advanced to attack left of enemy's position at Cingolo Hill, West Yorkshires forming the first line.

On arriving at the base of Cingolo, Major Fry commanding, the leading ½ Battalion formed up on a spur of the hill and opened fire on the Boers; the line was then successfully prolonged to the right by Head Quarters under Colonel Kitchener.

The 2nd Devons and the Queen's (the latter were wide of the Boers' left flank) advanced to crest of ridge, then wheeling to their left moved along the crest, the Boers retiring at once on their flank being turned.

During this time the Boers opened with shrapnel on the position occupied by the Regiment. Bivouacked on the position. G and H Companies employed during the night in dragging 64th Battery R.F.A. to a position whence they could shell Monte Christo the next day.

CASUALTIES.

KILLED (2 Men).

No. 5504 Pte. Hague, W.
„ 4782 Pte. Mathers, H. (died of wounds).

WOUNDED (10 Men).

February 18th.—2nd Brigade assaulted Monte Christo, *i.e.*, extreme left of Boer position. The Queen's advanced on right from top of Cingolo Mountains, West Yorkshires on left from bivouac of previous evening. First line commanded by Major Fry, B Company (Captain Berney), F Company (Major Watts), formed the firing line; C Company (Captain Carey), E Company (Major Heigham) in support; remainder of Battalion forming reserve under Colonel Kitchener. 2nd Devons formed second line, East Surrey Regt. Brigade Reserve. The advance was made practically without loss until the neck between Cingolo and Monte Christo was reached. B Company on the right and F Company on left at once advanced up the hill against the crest under cover of Artillery fire and long range Infantry volleys. B Company attacked direct up a precipitous slope overlooking the Boer laager. E Company was formed to the left in the neck, and together with Machine Guns kept up a heavy fire trying to quell fire from Boer laager. C Company rapidly reinforced B Company on crest of the hill.

The Boers retired to a further position along the ridge behind a reef of rocks. Captain Berney was killed whilst gallantly leading his Company to the assault. Colonel Kitchener rapidly brought up the remainder of the Battalion, and by prolonging the line to the right quickly drove the Boers from their second position, and charging across the plateau on summit of the hill occupied the crest overlooking the Boer laager, on which a heavy fire was opened.

The Queen's were at this time clearing the eastern slopes of the hills, and the 2nd Devons came up and prolonged our line to the right. The Boers for some time opened a very heavy shell fire on summit of hill and on shoulder occupied by F Company, under cover of which Boers in laager fled just as 4th Brigade advanced. By this time the whole Boer force was in full flight towards bridge over Tugela.

½ Battalion bivouacked on hill for the night, Head Quarters and remaining ½ Battalion returning to neck, as there was a difficulty of water supply.

CASUALTIES.

KILLED.

Officer.

Captain T. Berney.

N.C.O.'s and Men.

No. 1144 Pte. Brass, W.
  ,, 5022 Pte. Vaughan, J.
  ,, 4726 Corpl. Silcock, J. (died of wounds).
  ,, 3199 Pte. Howitt, A.

2nd Lieuts. Gretton and Porch and 40 Men wounded.

February 19th.—Head quarters returned to summit of Monte Christo, and day spent in road making and entrenching.

February 20th.—Moved down hill and bivouacked on east slope of Hlangwaini in centre of Boer laager.

February 21st.—Moved down to southern bank of Tugela under Colenso and bivouacked.

February 22nd.—At 2 a.m. crossed Tugela by pontoon bridge and bivouacked on open plain east of Fort Wylie. About 7 a.m. Boers shelled but did no damage, Brigade moving under shelter of Fort Wylie. Bathed at 1 p.m., and then advanced and took up position on ridge covering Guns and Howitzers. Spent night entrenching.

February 23rd.—Colonel Kitchener appointed to Command 11th Brigade, Major Fry assumes command of the Battalion. Boers shell position hard all day, our Guns replied vigorously. No casualties.

During afternoon General Hart advanced and captured position over Tugela Falls. At dusk we advanced and moved along railway and relieved 11th Brigade in a defensive position, ½ Battalion reserve.

February 24th.—Ordered to join General Hart's Force, who had lost seriously the previous day in attempting to take Hart's Hill. B, G, and H Companies remained in trenches as they could not be withdrawn, enemy's fire being so heavy. Remainder of the Battalion proceeded along the river bank to the Tugela

Falls and joined General Hart's Brigade at 8 p.m. Boers attack bivouac of 60 Rifles but were driven off; Battalion ordered at once to take up a position from left of bivouac to Pom-pom Bridge, covering Boer foot-bridge across the river. It was pitch dark at the time, so this was done by deploying the 5 Companies in line with fixed bayonets.

February 25th.—Same place. Armistice during day to bury dead and collect wounded. Time spent in burying the dead horses and making bivouac sanitary. At 8 p.m., shortly after conclusion of armistice, Boers opened a very heavy fire on the position.

February 26th.—Remained in same place; outposts during these days were very heavy, 2 Companies being on by day and the whole 5 by night. Casualties, 22nd to 26th, 11 Men wounded.

February 27th.—B, G, and H Companies, who joined us at 6-30 a.m. under Major Heigham, had been under heavy shell fire with Hildyard's Brigade but had escaped casualties.

Orders received at 7 a.m. to join Colonel Kitchener's Brigade (11th). The main Boer position was to be attacked, the general scheme being as follows:—

General Barton's Brigade was to attack Green Hill on the left of the Boers' position; Colonel Kitchener to attack Pieter's Hill in the centre; and Colonel Norcott's Brigade the hill on the Boer right (Hart's Hill), which General Hart had attempted a few days ago; the various attacks to be developed in the above order.

The Regiment was detailed for the firing line. D and F Companies led the Battalion and commenced the attack under the cover of very skilful shelling by Field Guns in position on the other bank of the river and within 2,300 yards of the Boer position. The railway was gained without opposition, D and F Companies under Major Watts took up position amongst rocks immediately over the railway, and brought a heavy fire to bear on Boers who were advancing to man trenches on hill to oppose Colonel Norcott's advance. A. B, C, and D prolonged the line to the right, working round the right shoulder of the hill as far as edge of wood. D and F Companies were then ordered to wheel to the right and advance straight up the hill, being joined by C, B, and G Companies as they passed.

The advance up the hill, led by Major Watts and Captain Mansel-Jones, was carried out in most gallant style. On arrival the Boers brought heavy shell fire to bear upon the hill; E Company was ordered to the right to hold railway and clear the donga between Pieter's Hill and Green Hill; this was done in good style and Boer fire from donga quelled.

As D and F Companies arrived at the top of the hill they came under a heavy cross fire from the hill on the left. Our left was promptly turned slightly back, and heavy volleys were poured into the Boers, who were standing up in their trenches, with excellent results.

This hill was immediately afterwards taken by Colonel Norcott's Brigade. The South Lancashire Regiment then came up on our left. The Boers appeared now to be in full retreat, but for a short time we were subjected to rather a heavy shell fire from 2 Field Guns and a Vickers-Maxim Quick-firing Gun. Rifle fire from a donga on right front also gave some trouble, but before dusk all was quiet.

CASUALTIES.

Officers.

Captain Mansel-Jones, Captain Tew, Lieuts. Spry, Pennell, V.C., and Boyall wounded.

KILLED.

N.C.O.'s and Men.

No. 1750 Sergt. Poplar, F.
,, 2105 Pte. Follon, C.
,, 5149 Pte. Smith, A. (died of wounds).
,, 3544 Pte. Freele, J.

and 25 wounded. 1 Martini-Maxim Gun was captured by the Regiment.

February 28th.—Bivouacked on heights overlooking the Tugela. Cavalry rode into Ladysmith.

March 1st.—Marched to Nelthorpe about 10 miles, where 2nd Division bivouacked. Officers permitted to ride into Ladysmith.

March 2nd.—Remained in bivouac at Nelthorpe.

March 3rd.—The Army marched through Ladysmith, the streets of which were lined by the Garrison. The Brigade passed through the town and bivouacked under Surprise Hill.

March 4th.—Tents arrived. Major Vowell arrives and assumes command of Battalion.

March 5th.—Remained in Camp.

March 6th.—Remained in Camp. Major Vowell leaves for Maritzburg to take duties of Press Censor.

March 7th.—Major Fry resumes command.

March 8th.—March to Modder Spruit, about eight miles north of Ladysmith, and camped for the night.

March 9th.—The whole Division marched to Sunday's River, about one mile in front of Elandslaagte.

March 10th.—Remained in Camp.

March 11th.—4 Companies under Major Heigham proceeded as escort to a Battery going to change its Guns at Modder Spruit, and returned to Camp about 4 p.m.

March 12th.—Remained in Camp.

March 13th.—Ditto.

March 14th.—Remained in Camp. News received of the capture of Bloemfontein.

March 15th.—Remained in Camp. 2nd Lieut. Ross rejoined from Hospital. Lieut. Lowe and 2nd Lieut. Shuttleworth, with a draft of 143 Men, arrived from England.

March 16th.—Remained in Camp.

March 17th.—Ditto.

March 18th.—Ditto.

March 19th.—2nd Lieut. E. Grant-Dalton joins from Maritzburg.

March 20th.—Remained in Camp.

March 21st.—Ditto.

March 22nd.—Ditto.

March 23rd.—Ditto.

March 24th.—Remained in Camp. General Clery resumes command of the Division.

March 25th.—Remained in Camp.

March 26th.—Colonel Kitchener (Brig. General) appointed to command 7th Brigade. Majors Fry and Heigham proceed to Durban on 14 days' sick leave. Major. Yale resumes command of the Battalion.

March 27th.—Shifted Camp to higher ground. Good deal of sickness in Camp (enteric and dysentery).

March 28th.—Remained in Camp.

March 29th.—Captain Wood and Lieut. Bousfield, with Volunteer Company (120 strong), join the Battalion.

March 30th.—Remained in Camp.

March 31st.—Ditto.

April 1st.—Ditto.

April 2nd.—Ditto.

April 3rd.—Band arrived.

April 4th.—Remained in Camp. News of the Koorn Spruit disaster received.

April 5th.—Inspection of baggage by G.O.C. Band instruments sent back.

April 6th.—Remained in Camp. Hospitals full. General Hunter's Division marches to Ladysmith.

April 7th.—Remained in Camp. Lieut. Porch returned to duty.

April 8th.—General Warren's Division arrived at Elandslaagte. General Hunter's Division proceeds to Orange Free State via Durban. Lieut. Boyall and 2nd Lieut. Barlow returned to duty. 2nd Lieut. Ross goes on sick leave.

April 9th.—Remained in Camp. News received of disaster to Irish Rifles near Bloemfontein.

April 10th.—Major Fry and Lieut. Pennell, V.C., rejoined; Major Fry resumes command. About 8-15 a.m., whilst at breakfast, the Boers suddenly opened shell fire on Camp, first shell passing just over the Mess and pitching in the East Surrey lines; others fell in quick succession about the Brigade Camp, Lieut. Crossman having a narrow escape, one shell pitching in his tent while he was in it.

The Brigade fell in and formed under cover of a rocky ridge. The Queen's, who were having a field day, were fortunately already in possession of an important kopje on the left of our defences. As soon as the Brigade was formed up, the West Yorkshires were ordered to occupy a kopje about three-quarters of a mile to the front of our position: ½ Battalion under command of Major Yale occupied the kopje in time to deny it to the Boers. Boers concentrated a heavy shell fire on this kopje at intervals throughout the day, and also long range rifle fire. Casualties very slight, owing to good natural cover being utilised, and not too many men being placed on kopje.

At dusk the Queen's and West Yorkshires were withdrawn from advanced position, and were ordered to entrench a position immediately in front of old Camp.

April 11th.—At 1 a.m. a general retirement took place to the Elandslaagte hills, where Force bivouacked for the remainder of the night.

CASUALTIES.

KILLED (1 Man).

No. 574 Pte. Loftus, J., B Company.

WOUNDED (6 Men).

About 8 a.m. sent out wagon under escort to fetch in baggage, &c., left in old Camp. Companies employed in entrenching.

April 12th.—Remained in bivouac. Pitched Camp in the afternoon. Boers occupied kopje which we vacated previous day, and shelled our Cavalry.

April 13th.—Remained in Camp. Entrenching.

April 14th.—At 2-30 a.m. Battalion warned to be ready to move at a moment's notice to join 10th Brigade. Boers supposed to be threatening our lines of Communication. At 7 a.m. Queen's and West Yorkshires march to a rendezvous about one mile off and remain there till 12 noon, when they returned to old site and pitched Camp.

April 15th.—Easter Sunday. Church Parade.

April 16th.—Employed all day making roads for Naval Guns.

April 17th.—At 5 a.m. marched to Pepworth's Farm, about 10 miles. Pitched Camp. A good deal of sickness (dysentery, &c.) in the Battalion.

April 18th.—At 6 a.m. marched to Surprise Hill, arrived there about 12 noon. Rain fell during the night and made the roads very heavy and difficult. On approaching Camp, General Kitchener rode out and met the Battalion, and was received with loud cheers.

April 19th.—Battalion marched to Klip River and bathed.

April 20th.—Usual Camp routine.

April 21st.—Heavy Guns heard in direction of Elandslaagte. At 10 a.m. Brigade fell in and marched about four miles out of Camp on Newcastle road, and halted, returning to Camp in the afternoon. Boers had been shelling Elandslaagte Collieries.

April 22nd.—Sunday Church Parade.

April 23rd.—Usual Camp routine.

April 24th.—Still in same Camp. General Warren given a command round the Cape side, and General Hildyard has taken over his Division. Colonel Hamilton, of the Queen's, takes over command of the 2nd Brigade.

Farewell order by Major-General Hildyard on relinquishing command of the 2nd Brigade:—

"Major-General Hildyard desires to convey to all ranks his keen appreciation of the good services rendered by them during the campaign in Natal. His experience of the several Battalions composing the Brigade when at Aldershot, during two training seasons, made him confident they would prove efficient in the field. At Willow Grange, at Colenso, at Vaal Krantz, and at Pieter's, they fully justified this expectation, and he will always recall with pride their conduct on these occasions.

The Major-General takes the opportunity of thanking C.O.'s for the support they have uniformly given him, and all Officers, W.O.'s, N.C.O.'s, and Men, for their excellent behaviour on all occasions. He sincerely regrets that his connection with the Brigade has now been severed, but confidently looks forward to hearing of fresh honours gained by it."

April 25th.—Lieut. Bicknell and 2nd Lieuts. Cuthell and Shuttleworth returned from sick leave.

April 26th.—Still at Surprise Hill. Major Watts went on, and Major Yale returned from, leave.

April 27th.—Usual Camp routine. G and H Companies played off their tie for Inter-company Football Challenge Shield. H Company won by two goals to nil.

April 28th.—Surprise Hill. F and E Companies played off their Football tie, F Company winning by two goals to one.

April 29th.—Surprise Hill. Sunday Church Parade. C and D Companies played off their tie in the afternoon, D Company winning.

April 30th.—Surprise Hill. General Kitchener and Staff came to dine. Smoking Concert afterwards.

May 1st.—Surprise Hill. A and B Companies played off their Football tie, A Company being the winners.

May 2nd.—Surprise Hill. K Company (Volunteers) played their Football tie against F Company, the latter winning easily.
The Queen's moved their Camp a-quarter of a mile west.

May 3rd.—Surprise Hill. Musketry carried out by Reservists and Militiamen of the Battalion.

May 4th.—Surprise Hill. Nothing worthy of note.

May 5th.—Surprise Hill. A and H Companies play off their Football tie, H winning by four goals to love.
Horse sickness made its appearance in the Regiment; lost one horse and one mule.

May 6th.—Surprise Hill. Sunday Church Parade.
Received orders to be in readiness to march to-morrow, 7 a.m.

May 7th.—Camp struck at 6 a.m. Battalion marched off at 7-40 a.m., forming head of main body; very pleasant march to Modder Spruit, which was reached at 11-30 a.m.; bivouacked for the night, tents being left behind; 4 Companies on outpost duty; evidently a general forward movement beginning. Received wire to say Major Yale sick on Hospital Ship "Trojan" with fever, leaving Captain Carey the Senior Officer after C.O.

May 8th.—Modder Spruit. Remained in bivouac all day long. Reveille sounding at 4-15 a.m., made the day a very long one. About mid-day the Queen's and the Devons moved out to the south-east in support of Lord Dundonald and Cavalry; presumably the remainder of Brigade join them to-morrow. News received that Lord Roberts has got to Vet River.

May 9th.—Bulwana Camp. Reveille at 4-15 a.m. The Brigade and Divisional Artillery marched about seven miles in a south-easterly direction. Battalion was escorted to the Guns. Bivouac reached about mid-day.

May 10th.—Bulwana Camp was left at 6 a.m., the Battalion forming head of main body. Arrived Sunday's River about mid-day, 11 miles' march, very dusty. On arrival found Dundonald's Cavalry Brigade, 60th and Scottish Rifles already here. Great scarcity of water; almost the only good water to be found was got by digging in the dry river bed. News reached that Lord Roberts only 10 miles from Kroonstadt, and Boers reported to be leaving Biggarsberg.

May 11th.—Sunday's River was left at 6-45 a.m. Right ½ Battalion, under Captain Carey, forming the advanced guard with the

Cavalry, remaining ½ Battalion formed head of main body. On approaching the Waschbank River the Cavalry came in touch with, and had one man wounded by, the enemy. Boers lit huge grass fires, extending for about 10 miles, either with the intention of spoiling our grazing area or showing they intended to make a stand. No news from the other side to-day.

May 12th.—Waschbank River. Battalion marched at 7 a.m., forming rear of main body, march 11 miles, covered by Cavalry, who saw about 80 Boers. On arriving in Camp great scarcity of water, making a move to-morrow a certainty. 2 Companies on outpost duty.

May 13th.—Vermaaks Kraal Farm was left at 7 a.m., Battalion forming part of main body. After going about four miles enemy dropped some shells into our baggage, but very quickly silenced by our Naval 12-pounders. At 11 a.m. Cavalry reported enemy on hills east of Vitock Farm. Brigade advanced in skirmishing order. Boers retired, their flanks being turned by Bethune's Horse, with 2 Guns, who had come up from Pomeroy. Enemy took up position north of Helpmakaar, and were vigorously shelled by us till nightfall. They returned our fire with 1 Gun, which, however, did little or no damage. Battalion bivouacked before Helpmakaar for the night, 3 Companies on outpost.

May 14th.—At dawn Helpmakaar was entered without opposition, the Regiment forming part of main body, enemy evidently fighting a rear-guard action. Horse Battery repeatedly came into action, causing enemy to retire before we could get within rifle range.

Reached Pieter's Farm at 1-30 p.m.; found there three Boers wounded by our shell fire in the morning. At 2-30 p.m. heavy Guns were heard to our left front, probably General Hildyard in action. Boers burning the whole country side.

May 15th.—Pieter's Farm was left at 6 a.m., the Battalion forming head of main body. Dundee was reached about 2-30 p.m. Town and Colliery a good deal damaged by the Boers' occupation.

March uninterrupted by the enemy, who had evidently retired in the night, some of their camp fires still smouldering; road very dusty and rather trying for the men. Recovered some drums in Dundee belonging to the Dublin Fusiliers and Royal Irish Rifles. Still no news from the Free State.

May 16th.—Dundee. Remained in bivouac for the day; rest very welcome to the Troops.

Congratulatory telegram received from the Queen as follows :—

" To General Sir Redvers Buller, V.C.,
            Dundee, Natal.

Delighted at your success and your entry into Dundee. Trust all wounded doing well.

V.R.I."

May 17th.—Dundee was left at 6-30 a.m., Force marched 14 miles and reached Danhauser at about 2 a.m. Two German Doctors (?) (Albrecht and Telemann) captured by one of our patrols and handed over to the Battalion for custody. They gave their paroles and lived in the Officers' Mess.

May 18th.—Danhauser was left at 4-45 a.m., the Battalion forming part of main body. A long halt was made at Ingagane in the middle of the day, and Newcastle was reached about 5-15 p.m. and entered without opposition; distance 23 miles. Marching and Men excellent. Town very pretty, but showed evident signs of Boer occupation.

May 19th.—Newcastle. Remained in bivouac just north of town. The 4th Brigade with some of Corps Troops moved on to Ingogo. Boers reported to be hard at work entrenching the Laing's Nek position.

May 20th.—Newcastle. Sunday Church Parade. The two German Doctors sent under escort to Ingogo.

May 21st. Newcastle. Queen's moved on to Ingogo, escorting some Guns. 3 Companies on outpost duty.

May 22nd.—Newcastle. A Squadron of Methuen's Mounted Infantry taken prisoners by the Boers, after making a good fight near Vryheid, one-third being killed, one-third wounded, and one-third prisoners. H Company played F for Inter-company Football Shield, H Company winning by two goals to love.

May 23rd.—Newcastle. Nothing worthy of note.

May 24th.—Newcastle. Queen's Birthday. H played D in the final for Company Shield, H Company winning by two goals to love.

May 25th.—Newcastle. 4 Companies on outpost duty. Rumours of the relief of Mafeking.

May 26th.—Newcastle. 5th Division under General Hildyard arrived. General Lyttelton's expected. Usual Camp routine.

May 27th.—Newcastle. Sunday Church Parade. Move to-morrow towards Ingogo, and 5th Division towards Utrecht. Official news received of the relief of Mafeking; Eloff and 120 Boer prisoners. Baden-Powell promoted Major-General.

May 28th.—Newcastle. Marched at 7 a.m., arrived about mid-day, very cold, making march pleasant. Bivouacked at Ingogo close to 3rd Bn. 60th Monument, of 1881.

4th Brigade moved about three miles to the front. Boers holding from Botha's Pass to Utrecht and Laing's Nek with about 5,000 men. About 4-30 p.m. Boers commenced shelling 4th Brigade with 6-inch Gun from Pugwana Hill; we replied with Naval 12-pounders, which fell short.

May 29th.—Ingogo. Remained in bivouac. Intermittent shelling went on all day, Boers replying with Long Tom from Pugwana Hill. 2 Companies on outpost duties.

Hildyard's Division reported to be at Utrecht. Boers observed throwing up works on our left flank. Sharp frost at night, weather beginning to be cold.

May 30th.—Ingogo. Nothing worthy of note.

May 31st.—Ingogo. Nothing to note. Awaiting news from the other side.

June 1st.—Ingogo. News received of Lord Roberts' entry into Johannesburg. Major Watts and Lieut. Francis returned from sick leave.

June 2nd.—Ingogo. Lord Roberts supposed to be half way to Pretoria. General Buller met Botha, presumably concerning surrender.

June 3rd.—Ingogo. Nothing to note. 3 Companies on outpost.

June 4th.—Ingogo. Still without tents. Nothing doing.

June 5th.—Ingogo. Armistice ended at 3-30 p.m., Boers deciding to fight it out. $\frac{1}{2}$ Battalion, under Major Watts, moved out half a mile to the right to protect General Buller's Head Quarters.

June 6th.—Right $\frac{1}{2}$ Battalion and Head Quarters joined the other $\frac{1}{2}$ Battalion. Desultory shelling, which continued most of the day. General Hildyard's Division took hill north-east of the bivouac (Van-Wyk), only 15 casualties. 3 Companies on outpost duty.

June 7th.—Ingogo. Usual shelling. 3 Companies on outpost. 11th Brigade to attack Botha's Pass to-morrow, supported by 2nd Brigade.

June 8th.—Ingogo. Reveille at 6 a.m. Battalion marched off at 9 a.m. to rendezvous at the Police Station on the Botha's Pass Road. At 11-30 p.m. attack on Inkelwaone commenced; the Devons on the left, the West Yorkshires on the right, formed the firing line; our right being protected by Lord Dundonald's Cavalry and A Battery R.H.A. The 11th Brigade simultaneously attacked Botha's Pass, the entire advance being covered by the heavy Guns on Van-Wyk. No opposition was met with until, after a very stiff climb, the crest was reached, when the enemy were seen to be holding the further crest line. D and B Companies formed the firing line under Major Watts. After some time the further crest was cleared by D and B Companies under a heavy Pom-pom, Maxim, and Rifle fire; B Company losing 2nd Lieut. E. Grant-Dalton hit in two places, one man killed and two wounded. Outposts were thrown out on the line gained by Battalion. Bivouacked on the position. The baggage being unable to get up the hill, a very cold and damp night was spent, a thick Scotch mist enveloping everything.

TOTAL CASUALTIES.
WOUNDED (1 Officer).

KILLED.

No. 5403 Pte. M. Flanaghan.

WOUNDED (3 Men).

June 9th.—Remainded all day in bivouac waiting for the baggage, which arrived in the evening. Weather very cold and cloudy.

Tents were collected from the Boer laager and used to shelter men of last draft, who had no warm clothing.

June 10th.—Battalion marched off about 7 a.m., forming head of main body in the direction of Gans-vlei. Enemy engaged by Cavalry and Horse Battery, which caused them to retire. A 14 mile march, passing through three countries:—Natal, Orange River Colony, and the Transvaal. Battalion bivouacked for the night at Gans-vlei.

June 11th.—Gans-vlei. Force marched at 11 a.m., 10th and 2nd Brigades to attack enemy, who were in position on Almonds Nek. Under cover of a very heavy Artillery fire, the position was taken at dusk. The 2nd Brigade on the left only had about 50 casualties, which were in the Queen's and East Surrey Regiment, who formed the firing line; 2nd West Yorkshires formed 2nd line, and did not come into action. Enemy only had 1 Gun and 1 Pom-pom, and these were put out of action almost at once. Battalion bivouacked for the night, 3 Companies on outpost duty. 2nd Lieut. Lupton (2nd Vol. Bn.) returned from sick leave.

June 12th.—Almonds Nek was left at 8 a.m., Battalion forming part of main body; marched to within four miles of Volksrust, where it bivouacked for the night. The rear guard of the enemy was once seen and a few shells were thrown at it by our heavy Guns; all Dutch farms flying the white flag.

June 13th.—Battalion started at 7 a.m. as head main body, and marched through Volksrust (the Dutch frontier town) to Charlestown (the English frontier) and bivouacked for the night. Officers' Mess established in a deserted house. Enemy evacuated Laing's Nek, which is reported to have been heavily entrenched, and nek occupied by General Clery. Boers supposed to be retreating on Lydenburg.

June 14th.—Charlestown. Tents having arrived, Camp was pitched for the first time since May 8th. Captain Carey went down to Durban on sick leave.

June 15th.—Charlestown. Nothing to note. 4 Companies on outpost duty.

June 16th.—Charlestown. East Surrey Regiment moved to Volksrust, to support General Hildyard, who moved towards Wakkerstroom. About half the Battalion visited Majuba Hill.

Trenches on Laing's Nek position somewhat extraordinary.

June 17th.—Charlestown. A very wet day. Lord Roberts reported to be having a big fight 18 miles from Pretoria.

June 18th.—Charlestown. Railway brought through Laing's Nek, and first train arrived at Volksrust. Lord Roberts reported successful. Probably march to-morrow.

June 19th.—Charlestown. Battalion, forming head main body, marched off at 8 a.m. and passed through Volksrust and bivouacked at Joubert's Farm (nine and a-half miles), where we were on the 12th inst.

June 20th.—Joubert's Farm. Marched at 8-15 a.m. in direction of Standerton. Uneventful march. Bivouacked at Zand's Spruit.
Small parties of Boers coming in daily and giving up their Arms. 3 Companies on outpost duty.

June 21st.—Zand's Spruit. Battalion was escort to the Supply Park. Marched off about 1 p.m. $\frac{1}{2}$ Battalion under Major Watts as rear guard. Very tedious march to Paarde Kop, last Company arriving at the bivouac at 12-30 a.m. (22nd inst.)

June 22nd.—Paarde Kop. Reveille at 3-45 a.m. Battalion marched off at 4-15 a.m. in rear of the Brigade. After marching 20 miles Camp was pitched near Kroonsdaai. Country very flat and weather intensely cold; sharp frosts every night. 1 Company on outpost duty.

June 23rd.—Kroonsdaai. Remained in Camp, everyone thankful for the day's rest. 1 Company on outpost duty.

June 24th.—Force marched at 8 a.m., Standerton being reached about mid-day, where Camp was pitched. Town very, very dirty, and it being Sunday the few shops there are were closed.

June 25th.—Standerton. Nothing doing, a quiet day in Camp.

June 26th.—Standerton. Still in Camp, repairing railway up to the bridge, which is blown up. 11th Brigade went back to Platrand to protect the line, as the telegraph line was cut last night. 1½ Companies on outpost duty.

June 27th.—Standerton. Boers coming in daily with Rifles and Ammunition. Force of Cavalry with Horse Battery sent out to reconnoitre. Rumours of a big fight at Middleburg. 1½ Companies on outpost duty.

June 28th.—Standerton. Very bad news, Major Hobbs reported to have been killed in action near Kroonstadt on his way down from Pretoria. The connecting rods (which had been hidden) of the 15 Engines captured at Standerton were found buried a-quarter of a mile down the line.

June 29th.—Standerton. Still in Camp. Battalion hard at work entrenching the outpost line. 2 Companies on outpost.

June 30th.—Standerton. 4th Brigade marched off about 8 a.m. in the direction of Heidelberg with a proportion of Guns and Corps Troops. 2 Companies on outpost.

July 1st.—Standerton. Sunday; miserable day, wet and cold. Lung sickness broken out amongst the oxen. 2 Companies on outpost duty.

July 2nd.—Standerton. Cattle were inoculated against lung sickness. Most of the Battalion were employed on the railway diversion.

July 3rd.—Standerton. Nothing worthy of note, very little news from the other side. 2 Companies on outpost.

July 4th.—Standerton. Battalion engaged in entrenching the kop, and working on the railway. 2 Companies on outpost.

July 5th.—Standerton. Still in Camp; still working on the railway deviation. 1½ Companies on outpost. Very cold night.

July 6th.—Standerton. Nothing worthy of note, very little news 1½ Companies on outpost.

July 7th.—Standerton. Ox transport to be exchanged for mule transport. 1½ Companies on outpost.

July 8th.—Standerton. Sunday Church Parade. Line reported cut between here and Greylingstadt. 2 Companies on outpost. ½ Battalion Devons went to Waterval.

July 9th.—Standerton. Remainder of Devons left, for Waterval. West Yorks. moved about one mile to Devons' old Camp. Officers' Mess established in a house. 2 Companies on outpost.

July 10th.—Standerton. Battalion hard at work entrenching new outpost line. 2 Companies on outpost.

July 11th.—Standerton. New bridge over river nearly broken last night by some Hollander (presumably) starting 10 trucks down the incline. Trucks smashed to pieces; luckily bridge hardly damaged at all. 2 Companies on outpost. Boers constantly attempting to damage line between here and Greylingstadt.

July 12th.—Standerton. 2nd Lieut. Gretton left for Durban with jaundice. Very sharp frost last night. Regimental Sports came off; several good races. Rundle reported to have occupied Bethlehem. 2 Companies on outpost.

July 13th.—Standerton. Bethune's Mounted Infantry reported to be engaged with enemy about four miles from here; supply train on its way back from Waterval was fired at, no casualties. 2 Companies on outpost.

July 14th.—Standerton. Regimental Sports held during the afternoon; very good racing. 2 Companies on outpost.

July 15th.—Standerton. Sunday Church Parade as usual. 2nd Lieut. Barlow played organ supplied by our Mess. 2 Companies on outpost.

July 16th.—Standerton. Received news this morning of the " Greys," 2 Horse Guns, and 5 Companies of the Lincolnshires being cut up in Nitral's Nek, near Pretoria. Garrison Sports held in the afternoon; much appreciated by all. The Regiment won the Mile, the

Quarter-mile, the 100 Yards, the old Soldiers', and the Obstacle Race, thus winning a good deal more than its share.

July 17th.—Standerton. Received news this morning of the burning of the Foreign Legations in China, probably meaning the dispatch of more Troops. Persistent rumours of the early departure for home of the 2nd Brigade as soon as De Wet and Steyn have given in. 2 Companies on outpost.

July 18th.—Standerton. News received of the capture of Tientsin by the allies. 1,500 Men and 5 Guns have got through Rundle's lines in the direction of Lindley. 2 Companies on outpost.

July 19th.—Standerton. Nothing worthy of note.

July 20th.—Standerton. ½ Battalion under Major Watts escorted Convoy to General Clery, and returned in the evening.

Major Heigham rejoined Battalion from Depôt. 2 Companies on outpost. Generals Clery and Hildyard made forward movement in conjunction with Roberts towards Bethel.

July 21st.—Standerton. Lines reported to be again cut. Each Great Power supposed to be sending 40,000 Troops to China.

China declares War against Russia. 2 Companies on outpost.

July 22nd.—Standerton. Battalion marched off in the middle of Divine Service to put out grass fire. 2 Companies on outpost.

July 23rd.—Nothing to note. Rained in the night, the first we have had for a long time. 2 Companies on outpost.

July 24th.—Standerton. Battalion exercised in manning the defences. General Hildyard reported to have driven Boers off Grass Kop. Dublins attacked near Katbosch Spruit; Boers driven off without loss. 2 Companies on outpost.

July 25th.—Standerton. No news of any sort. 2 Companies on outpost.

July 26th.—Standerton. General Hildyard reported to be again engaged. 2 Companies on outpost.

July 27th.—Standerton. General French reported to be only eight miles from Middleburg. Roberts at Balmoral. 2 Companies on outpost.

July 28th.—Standerton. Captain Mansel-Jones awarded the V.C. for gallant leading at Railway Hill, February 27th, 1900. News received of the surrender near Kroonstadt of General De Wet with 500 men. 2 Companies on outpost.

July 29th.—Standerton.—Usual Church Parade. Rumours of a move to-morrow. 2 Companies on outpost.

July 30th.—Standerton. B, C, D, and E Companies, with Regiment Head Quarters, paraded at 4-30 a.m., and proceeded about seven miles up the line by train, together with 4 Companies of the Queen's and 4 of the East Surreys. On leaving the train we were met by the M. I. and 2 Howitzers, 1 F.B.R.A., and 1 5-inch Gun.

The idea was to surround, if possible, a small Commando 300 strong, who had been located on Joubert's Kop. The enemy had evidently been apprised of our move and had moved all their wagons at early dawn. Joubert's Kop was occupied without resistance, and our Cavalry came in touch with enemy, who were holding a line of ridges about one and a-half miles south of Joubert's Kop. The Howitzers and Field Batteries came into action and the Infantry deployed for attack; the West Yorkshires on the right, and the Queen's on the left, and the East Surreys in reserve; but after the Guns had fired a few rounds the enemy retired. South of Verde Road a small laager was captured, and about 300 sacks of mealies and a lot of Ammunition destroyed. The Battalion marched home, having done about 25 miles during the day, getting into Camp about 6 p.m. The marching of the Men was excellent. News received of the surrender of Prinsloo with 5,000 Men and 18 Guns to Hunter at Bethlehem.

July 31st.—Standerton. Roberts reported to be at Machadodorp. Two farms, suspected of signalling to enemy, searched late at night, with the result that two natives and four horses were captured. 2 Companies on outpost.

August 1st.—Standerton. English Mail arrived. 2 Companies on outpost.

August 2nd.—Standerton. 2 Companies on outpost. In the afternoon C Company under Captain Carey proceeded to Katbosch Spruit as escort to a Supply Park.

August 3rd.—Standerton. A, B, and G Companies, under the command of Major H. E. Watts, started at 4-30 a.m. with 4 Companies of the Queen's, under Colonel Pink, to support our Mounted Troops, who were to burn some farmhouses south of Standerton. The Mounted Troops and Guns became engaged: the farms were destroyed and the Force returned to Camp about 5 p.m. C Company returned from Katbosch Spruit about 4-30 p.m. 2 Companies on outpost.

August 4th.—Standerton. News received of the death of the Duke of Edinburgh, and the assassination of King Humbert of Italy. 3 Companies on outpost.

August 5th.—Standerton. Confirmation of the capture by Hunter and Ian Hamilton of 5,000 Boers and Guns. Train overturned and burnt by enemy near Honing Spruit. Church Parade as usual. 3 Companies on outpost.

August 6th.—Standerton. No news. Rumours of a possible move to Heidelberg. 3 Companies on outpost.

August 7th.—Standerton. Orders received in the afternoon to be prepared to entrain for Pretoria at once. Camp immediately struck and all preparations, when the order was countermanded. K Company under Captain Wood escorted some Guns to Heidelberg and returned in the evening. 2 Companies on outpost duty.

August 8th.—Standerton. Battalion with first line of transport commenced entraining at 5 a.m.; right ½ Battalion started at 7-45 a.m., left ½ under Major Heigham left two hours later. Uneventful journey to Elandsfontein, when telegram was received changing our destination from Pretoria to Krugersdorp, at which place, after a long wait at Johannesburg, the first train arrived at 10-30 p.m., the second at midnight; General Barton was in command at Krugersdorp. An issue of rum was given to the Men, who were very tired by the long journey in open trucks. The Battalion bivouacked ½ in the trucks and ½ on the platform. Orders received to proceed to Blaaubank in the morning.

August 9th.—Krugersdorp. Train started at 6 a.m. and reached Randfontein at 7 a.m., where we were joined by 2 Howitzers, 40 1. Yeomanry, 40 E.P.H., and about 100 C.I.V., and details, the whole under the command of Major Fry. The line being reported clear we started off, the Howitzers by road with the Yeomanry scouting in front, and the train keeping pace with the Guns. Randfontein was left at about 1 p.m. and Blaaubank was reached about 6 p.m. without incident. On arrival we found some K.S.L.I., 2 15-pounders, C.I.V., and I.Y.; General Smith-Dorrien was in command. 1 Company on outpost.

August 10th.—Blaaubank. Quiet morning in Camp. Transport for the Battalion wired for from Krugersdorp. The 2 15-pounders, K.S.L.I., the C.I.V.'s, and the I.Y. left in the evening for a point some 10 miles down the line, the Battalion being left alone. 2 Companies on outpost. During the night the Convoy, escorted by I.Y., arrived from Krugersdorp. Night passed without anything occurring.

August 11th.—Blaaubank. ½ Battalion, under Major Heigham, consisting of A, B, C, and D Companies, entrained at 7 and started about 9 to join the Force down the line; Major Fry left in command at Blaaubank by General Smith-Dorrien. Very busy day. Signallers got in touch with Lord Kitchener's Column. Remaining ½ Battalion and Regimental Head Quarters started for Welverdiend about 6 p.m., as escort for Convoy. Uneventful march; arrived at Welverdiend about 12-30 a.m., 17 miles' march, joining the remaining ½ Battalion, and bivouacked for the remainder of the night. Lord Kitchener's Column had also arrived during the day; Force mainly composed of Cavalry.

August 12th.—Welverdiend. Whole Force marched about 9 a.m. ½ Battalion as rear guard under Major Heigham. Marched about 12 miles over rather rough country till a spruit was reached, which caused so much delay that the Force bivouacked on other side for the night. Methuen's Guns heard during the day, and he is reported to have captured 1 of De Wet's Guns and 2 Ammunition Wagons. Weather windy and rather cold, but considerably warmer than Natal. Rumour that Buller has had a successful fight against Botha.

August 13th.—Force marched at 3-30 a.m. in same order as yesterday. after hasty breakfast. Marched 25 miles in a northerly direction. Extremely trying march as the halts were most irregular, and no food for 13 hours. When Camp was reached at 4-30 p.m., many men fell out in the leading ½ Battalion from exhaustion alone, consequent of the lack of food. The rear ½ Battalion did not arrive in the bivouac until 4-30 a.m. The bivouac was Swartz Kop.

August 14th.—Swartz Kop. After a good night's rest, which we were all very much in want of, the Force started at 6 a.m. for Waterval (15 miles). The Battalion formed the advance guard. Waterval was reached without incident at about 2 p.m. De Wet reported to have got through Majato's Pass and gone north, consequently chase abandoned. Bivouacked for the night. 1 Section on outpost. 60 sick sent back in the morning with a returning Convoy, with Captain Carey in command.

August 15th.—Waterval. Force marched at 9 a.m. Head Quarters ½ Battalion forming head of Infantry Column, remaining ½ Battalion under Major Heigham still with baggage. Uneventful march to Leefontein (15 miles), reached at 5 p.m. Battalion marched excellently. 1 Section on outpost. Country quite full of game, one buck secured on the march. 5th Fusiliers marched through Waterval early in the morning.

August 16th.—Leefontein. The left ½ Battalion joined Head Quarters late last night, having had a very tiring day with the baggage, and only their biscuit rations issued to them.
Force marched at 4 a.m., the Battalion forming part of main body, with the intention of relieving Colonel Hare and 300 Bushmen, who had been held up by the enemy for nearly a fortnight near Brakfontein. On reaching the latter place the Force was reported relieved, and the Battalion bivouacked for the night. The country we were now in was more cultivated and had far more farms than usual; orange groves most refreshing. The Battalion marched excellently this last week, although the men were soft from staying so long at Standerton, indeed at one time the Battalion accomplished 75 miles in 72 hours. The horses of the Mounted Troops are in a deplorable condition, numbers being left on the roadside every day.

August 17th.—Brakfontein. The Force remained all day in the bivouac, a rest which was most welcome to man and beast. Colonel Hare with 300 Colonials had held the kopje near Brakfontein against 3,000 Boers and 7 Guns for 12 days, losing all his horses and cattle and 70 Men killed and wounded.
The enemy retired yesterday on hearing of our approach. Weather getting quite hot again, and the country much more cultivated and more wooded, being watered by the Elands River. 1 Company on outpost.

August 18th.—Brakfontein was left at 4-30 a.m., the Battalion forming the advanced guard, and marched some 15 miles to

Twee River, which was reached about 4-30 p.m.   At Ebenezer
we passed Lord Methuen's Force, which was on its way to
Zeerust, thereby meeting the 1st Battalion 5th Fusiliers, who
were attached to the 14th for so long at Aldershot. The
marching of the Men was very good; the country very pretty,
it being the commencement of Spring, and the weather all that
could be desired.   1 Company on outpost duty.   Our present
destination supposed to be Pretoria, which is five days' march
off.

August 19th.—Twee River was left at 4-15 a.m.   Battalion formed
head of main body and marched to Rustenburg, passing through
Majato's Pass, where a halt of 20 minutes was made. Rustenburg
was reached at about 12-30 p.m., a distance of about 16 miles.
Here the Force bivouacked for the night.

August 20th.—Rustenburg.   Battalion, forming the rear guard,
marched off at 5 a.m. Rustenburg, rather pretty village, clean,
and well kept; very few men in the village, as the day we arrived
they had trekked to the neighbouring hills. The Force marched
about 12 miles, when Battalion bivouacked for the night at
Klipfontein.

Numerous drifts were crossed on the way.   The Town Hall of
Rustenburg was searched by 1 Company, and six sacks of ammunition found and destroyed.   Horses and mules in very bad condition
from want of forage, which had completely run out.

August 21st.—Klipfontein was left at 2-30 a.m., Battalion forming
advanced guard. Most of the early morning was spent crossing
drifts, about two miles from Camp. After going about 14 miles,
the Force halted at 11 a.m. and rested until 3 p.m., when a start
was made for Wolhuters Kop, which was reached at 6 p.m., the
total distance marched being 24 miles. Marching of Men was
excellent, very few falling out. Some little excitement was
caused on nearing the kop by a few Boers being seen, two of
whom (De Wet's Scouts) were captured by our M.I. 1 Company
on outpost duty.

August 22nd.—Wolhuters Kop. Battalion was supposed to march
with rest of Force to Commando Nek at 5-30 a.m., but at the
last moment the Battalion, with K.S.L.I. and 1 Section R.F.A.
and the M.I., the whole under General Smith-Dorrien, were
detached to march to Beeste Kraal (distance about 25 miles) to
block the drifts of Crocodile River against De Wet, who was
supposed to be marching north-west, trying to break away west;
Lord Kitchener with remainder of Force moved to Commando
Nek, en route to Pretoria.

Battalion, with Smith-Dorrien's Force, marched to Koos-
Managali, about 12 miles, which was reached about 1-15 p.m.
The place consisted of a native reservation among some broken
kopjes. 1 Company on outpost.

August 23rd.—Koos-Managali. At 2 p.m. General Dorrien heard by
Dispatch Rider from Lord Roberts that De Wet had undoubtedly

gone north of Pretoria, so that there was no need of a Force at Crocodile River. Consequently, at 5-30 a.m., the Force returned to the previous night's bivouac at Wolhuters Kop, Battalion forming the rear guard ; bivouac was reached at 12-30 p.m. 1 Company on outpost.

August 24th.—Wolhuters Kop was left at 5-30 a.m., the Battalion again forming the advanced guard, and after an easy march of about 12 miles through Commando Nek, reached Rietfontein at noon. Commando Nek was held by the Border Regt., and further on the Yorkshire Light Infantry were passed near the Nek, where the Lincolns and "Greys" were cut up a few weeks previously. To-morrow we march into Pretoria. 1 Company on outpost.

August 25th.—Rietfontein was left at 5-30 a.m., ½ Battalion forming main body, left ½ forming rear guard. Pretoria was reached about mid-day, after a march of 15 miles, during which Wonderboom Fort was passed on our left. The Battalion bivouacked on the Race Course for the night. Pretoria not a very imposing place ; smaller than one would expect. Rumours of an early move to Belfast, where a big battle is to be fought ; Buller and Roberts both there.

August 26th.—Pretoria. Battalion ordered to entrain for Belfast at noon, but order suddenly countermanded as everything was being got ready.

Major Fry appointed second in command. Lieut. H. S. Pennell, V.C., obtained his Company in his own Regiment.

The following letter received from General Hamilton, 2nd Brigade, begins :—

" My dear Fry,

"I did not have a chance of saying a few words to your Regiment before you left, for I was away the previous day, and the Railway Station was not a good place for me to say what I wanted.

" Will you please let all the Regiment know how sorry I am to lose them out of my Brigade. I have known the West Yorkshires long enough now to appreciate the good stuff there is in them, and I can truly say I don't wish to have a better Regiment on service.

" With me, I have always had a feeling that the West Yorkshires could be relied on to do whatever they were asked to do. I don't give up all hope of seeing you in the Brigade again, although I fear we are stuck here for the present.

" We may be relieved by some other Troops from the Orange River Colony. No one will be better pleased than I to welcome you back, should we get into Pretoria ; in the meantime I wish you all success.

" Yours sincerely,
" E. S. HAMILTON."

2

Captain Carey and 2nd Lieut. Barlow returned with sick who were sent back to Krugersdorp. Lieut. Francis, with details which were left at Standerton, arrived.

August 27th.—Pretoria. A, B and C and E Companies, under Major Heigham and Captain Carey respectively, entrained early this morning and started for Belfast. Battalion supposed to follow them, but only G and ½ H Companies managed to get away in the afternoon. Bivouacked for the night at the station. Very dusty and dirty. Plenty of rolling stock, but very few engines.

August 28th.—Pretoria. Still at the station waiting. The first line of transport, with animals, &c., and a few men of H Company with Lieuts. Francis and Crossman, managed to get away this morning. Oliver and 500 men reported captured. De Wet again escaped south. While the Battalion was on the march with Lord Kitchener's Column all Lord Roberts' proclamations were withdrawn, and in future all burghers are to be treated as prisoners of war. The remainder of the Battalion and Head Quarters, less 30 Men and Lieut. Bousfield of K Company, left at 4-30 p.m. for Belfast. Middleburg was not reached till 4-30 a.m., 29th inst. During the latter part of the night and early morning it rained very heavily, making it very miserable for the Men, who were in open trucks.

August 29th.—Middleburg. On arrival at Middleburg, found Lieuts. Francis and Crossman with transport, who had left Pretoria by a previous train. One of their trucks with first line of transport broke down, and was left at Oliphants River. Both trains remained at Middleburg all day long, as an engine had left the rails, and further up the line two trains had collided, causing a few casualties. Machadodorp reported to have been taken by the British after some heavy fighting, Rifle Brigade capturing a Pom-pom, and French two more, with several wagons loaded with Ammunition.

The Men were all entrained again at 10 p.m., but the train did not leave until 4-45 a.m., 30th inst.

August 30th.—Middleburg was left at 4-45 a.m. Belfast was reached at 8-30 a.m., where Major Heigham and remainder of Battalion were found. Battalion bivouacked close to the railway line. 5 Companies detached—2 in town and 3 about two miles away. Apparently we are to remain here until the K.S.L.I. arrive to make up General Smith-Dorrien's Brigade, which is to consist of the West Yorkshires, the K.S.L.I., Gordon Highlanders, and the Royal Scots. Lord Roberts visited the Officers' Mess during the day.

August 31st.—Belfast. In bivouac all day near the station. 5 Companies under Major Heigham on detachment about one and a-half miles out, finding the outposts, &c. Belfast town consists of the usual small collection of tin houses, hardly any Dutchmen living there.

2A

September 1st.—Belfast. Remained in Camp near the station. The K.S.L.I. arriving in detachments from Pretoria. The day spent in building shelters of corrugated iron for the Men.

September 2nd.—Belfast. Sunday. Orders received at 12 o'clock last night for the Battalion with Brabant's Horse to proceed via Machadodorp and Helvitia to Elands Spruit, to escort a Convoy to General Buller. The Force started at 10-30 a.m., and marched to Dalmanutha, where a halt of an hour was made. Dalmanutha was left at 4 p.m. and Machadodorp was reached at 7 p.m., where the Battalion bivouacked for the night (18 miles' march).

September 3rd.—Machadodorp. Orders suddenly received cancelling our march, and ordering Brabant's Horse back to Dalmanutha. Machadodorp is the usual small and dirty Dutch town, surrounded by long range of hills, and little or no grazing for the cattle, which are in a terribly poor condition, numbers having to be shot on every march. Orders received about 10 a.m. for Battalion to proceed with Convoy to Helvitia. After a short march of about six miles over very hilly country, Helvitia was reached about 5-30 p.m.

September 4th.—Helvitia was left about 6 a.m. and the Battalion, still acting as escort to Convoy, reached Schuman's Drift, after a short but hilly march of about six miles, about mid-day; there the Convoy was handed over to an escort sent out by General Bu ler, who had been stopped by a very strong position about five miles away.

Battalion bivouacked for the night about one and a-half miles away from ½ Battalion of the Inniskilling Fusiliers; many small parties of the enemy in the neighbouring hills. This morning a signalling post of the Inniskillings was rushed by a small party of the Boers under the very nose of the ½ Battalion. 2 Companies on outpost, 2 Companies on guard over Convoy.

September 5th.—Schuman's Drift was left at 6 a.m. by the leading Companies of the Battalion which was to escort back to Helvitia the now empty Convoy. The leading Companies reached Helvitia again, after an easy march of about six miles, without incident. Battalion bivouacked for the night.

September 6th.—Helvitia. B and G Companies paraded at 4-15 a.m. and picqueted half of the road to Machadodorp; remainder of Battalion left Helvitia at 7-30 a.m. After marching about three miles B and G Companies were picked up, and the Battalion turned off sharply to the left and reached Waterval Boven about 2 p.m.

On its arrival the Garrison (2 Companies Coldstream Guards) was relieved, and the Battalion bivouacked for the night just outside the town. 2 Companies on outpost.

September 7th.—Waterval Boven. Very cold and misty day. 3 Companies took up quarters in the town—1 in the club-house and the 2 others in the railway offices—where the Men were very comfortable. Major Fry Commandant of the town, which is very prettily situated on the Crocodile River, with large ranges of hills all round, making it a very difficult matter to get supplies up to the outposts.

General Pole-Carew's Division (11th) camped on the hills north-west of the town. The only Troops in the Garrison besides the West Yorkshires are some 60 M.I. 2 Companies on outpost.

September 8th.—Waterval Boven. D and H Companies with M.I. sent out to get touch with Colonel Henry's Force, which was operating some miles south of the town, returning to Camp in the evening. 1 more Company sent out on detachment about one and a-half miles south-west of town.

General Buller reported to be in Lydenburg with his Force. Officers' Mess once more established in a house close to the railway, tin shelters being erected for the Companies. Bivouacked outside the town. Town being generally cleaned up and houses visited and occupants sent away to Pretoria. 2nd Lieut. Lyster appointed Assistant Provost Marshal. 3 Companies on outpost.

September 9th.—Waterval Boven. Sunday. Rev. Wainman held divine service of all Troops quartered in or near the town.

Colonel Henry's Guns heard during most of the day, and reported to be most successful. Same outposts.

September 10th.—Waterval Boven. 2 more Companies left the town to bivouac under shelters at tactical points. Received orders about noon to hold ourselves in readiness to march to Machadodorp to join General Hutton's Command. Same outposts.

September 11th.—Waterval Boven. Received orders to move at 7-30 a.m., and Battalion marched off about 10 a.m. and arrived at Machadodorp about 5 p.m., after a nine miles' march. The transport did not arrive till very late, the oxen being absolutely done, several dying on the road. No news of any sort, and, still worse, no mail, making it a fortnight since we received the last one. The Convoy we were to have escorted to General Hutton was sent early this morning with only 25 Men as escort. They were held up by the Boers about nine miles out. A Squadron of the 7th Dragoon Guards and 2 Companies of the Liverpools were sent out to-night to relieve them, and the West Yorkshires are to go on to-morrow and take the Convoy on to General Hutton. 1 section on outpost duty.

September 12th.—Machadodorp. At 5-30 a.m. mule transport (a very wretched looking lot) was handed over to the Battalion instead of the ox wagons, and the Battalion marched off at 6-30 a.m. After a very uphill march of about nine miles, the Convoy was reached about 10-30 a.m. and the mid-day halt was made. Apparently the Convoy had taken the wrong road and about three miles from here were fired on, so they retired here, where there was a farm (Rensburg's Farm) and plenty of water. Owing to our Regimental transport being in such a poor condition it was impossible to proceed any further, so a halt was made for the night. 2 Companies on outpost duty.

September 13th.—Rensburg's Farm was left by the Battalion at 6 a.m. and marched to Elands Hoek, where General Hutton had had his Camp, which was reached at 11 a.m. after a very hilly march of about 10 miles. After trying in vain to get into Communication with General Hutton's Column, Major Heigham with K and A Companies proceeded to a point about four miles on, which was reached after dark; B Company was left to hold section of road between here and Rensburg's Farm; remainder of Battalion bivouacked for the night.

September 14th.—Elands Hoek. H Company was sent back with the now empty Convoy to hold the ridge overlooking Rensburg's Farm, and guard our Communication with Machadodorp. C Company under Captain Carey was left at last night's bivouac to fulfil similiar duties. Remainder of Battalion marched at 6-30 a.m. to join Major Heigham's Company, which was reached about 9 a.m. Here all Companies, excepting F and G, were detached to hold the neighbouring hills, the whole Battalion thereby protecting Noctegedacht and the railway line. Country generally very hilly and rugged, and absolutely impracticable for wheeled transport.

September 15th.—Noctegedacht. Remained in bivouac. News received of General French's entry into Barberton. General opinion that the War will end very soon. Some Companies on detachment.

September 16th.—Noctegedacht. Battalion ordered to march to Machadodorp, and left about 1 p.m. Elands Hoek was reached about 5 p.m., where the Battalion bivouacked for the night. 1 Company on outpost.

September 18th.—Noctegedacht. Elands Hoek. A, C, G, and K Companies under Major Watts started for Machadodorp at 6 a.m., remainder of the Battalion waiting to bring in captured cattle and prisoners, bivouacking there for another night, which proved to be horribly wet; everything was soaked.

September 19th.—Elands Hoek. After a very wet night, a thick wetting Scotch mist prevailed till about 10 a.m., when the sun managed to get through. The remaining 3 Companies, D, E, and A, with Battalion Head Quarters, left the Hoek at 9-30 a.m., and B Company's post at Veltrered was reached at 11 a.m., the Men marching in their great coats on account of the extra weight of the wet blankets on the wagons. Here a halt was made till 12-30 p.m., when Battalion marched, leaving B Company behind with stores, &c., through to H Company's post, near Rensburg's Farm, which was reached about 2-30 p.m., after a march of about 10 miles. Battalion bivouacked for the night.

September 20th.—Rensburg Farm. B Company arrived about mid-day with remainder of baggage and stores, and the 5 Companies, which were marched at 1 p.m., for Machadodorp. Before starting, a message was received, stating Battalion ordered to entrain for

Pretoria. All sorts of conjectures as to reason for going there, the two more popular ones being either home or De Wet.

Machadodorp was reached about 5 p.m., and the Battalion bivouacked for the night with the exception of 4 Companies who had been sent on under Major Watts.

September 21st.—Machadodorp. Remained in bivouac all day long, waiting for train to convey us to Pretoria, where we are to form a Brigade with the Argyll and Sutherland Highlanders, under General Cunningham, for the purpose of operating in the Rustenburg district.

September 22nd.—Machadodorp. D Company with Regimental Head Quarters entrained at 4 a.m., Pretoria being reached at 11 p.m., where Troops bivouacked for remainder of the night in the station yard. At Elands River, which was reached about 6-30 p.m., there was great excitement, as Commando under General Erasmus had shelled the station in the morning, but doing little damage and only killing one man. It subsequently transpired that General Paget, hearing of what was going on, did a night march of 26 miles, and captured and burned their laager while they were away, seizing a number of wagons, oxen, &c.

September 23rd.—Pretoria. After an uneventful journey H and ½ Battalion arrived in the morning under Major Watts, and at 3-30 p.m. the 3 Companies were moved to a bivouac near Daaspoort, to the north of the town. No further news, but De Wet and De la Rey still at large.

September 24th.—Pretoria. G, K, F, and remainder of B Companies arrived from Machadodorp without incident; no news of any sort.

September 25th.—Pretoria. Late last night E Company arrived from Machadodorp, and ½ A Company a little later.

September 26th.—Pretoria. Still in bivouac; very windy and dusty; ½ Company with 1st line Regimental transport arrived from Machadodorp.

September 27th.—Pretoria. Battalion marched at 6 a.m. as advanced guard, and 2 Guns Elswick Battery and 75th Field Battery Royal Artillery and the Argyll and Sutherland Highlanders to Rietfontein, 16 miles, which was reached about 2 p.m., after a rather tiring march. Lieut. Francis was left at Pretoria to bring on remainder of transport. Major Heigham and ½ C Company still to arrive from Machadodorp. The Brigade is to act as support to General Clements' and General Broadwood's Columns. 1 Section on outpost duty.

September 28th.—Rietfontein was left at 6-15 a.m., Battalion forming rear guard and escort to baggage, and marched about 11 miles to Bokfontein, which was reached about 11 a.m. Bivouacked for the night. 1½ Companies on outpost duty

September 29th.—Bokfontein was left at 6 a.m., Battalion forming advanced guard, and marched to Elands Kraal (about 12 miles), which was reached about 11-30 a.m. after a hot, but otherwise pleasant, march. Broadwood reported to be at Rustenburg, and a Commando (1,000 strong) reported about 10 miles away to our right. 1 Company on outpost.

September 30th.—Elands Kraal. Force marched at 6-30 a.m. Battalion forming part of main body and rear guard marched to Krondalstadt (about 11 miles) through rather hilly and wooded country; being springtime, country generally very pretty one. 1 Company on outpost.

October 1st.—Krondalstadt. Battalion marched off at 6 a.m., forming advanced guard. About two miles from Rustenburg, General Clements' Force crossed on line of march, causing us a long delay, Rustenburg not being reached until 5-30 p.m. The force bivouacked just outside the town. General Broadwood's Force, which had been holding the place, left as soon as we arrived. 1 Company on outpost.

October 2nd.—Rustenburg. G and H Companies, with 2 Field Guns and 2 Companies Argyll and Sutherland Highlanders, marched back about 13 miles to burn some farms, near which two unarmed Highlanders had been sniped at and killed the previous day. 1 Company on outpost.

October 3rd.—Rustenburg. G and H Companies returned about midday, having destroyed the farms and meeting with no opposition. News received that Lord Roberts appointed Commander-in-Chief and of the C.I.Vs.' departure for home, and the Guards returning from Koomati Poort, all pointing to the practical conclusion of the War. 1 Company on outpost.

October 4th.—Rustenburg. A, B, D, and E Companies under Major Watts paraded at 6 a.m., and with 2 Guns started for Wolhuters Kop, there to meet a Convoy, and escort it back to Rustenburg. 1 Company on outpost.

October 5th.—Rustenburg. Methuen's Division camped near Oliphant's Nek, nearly 12 miles away. Broadwood's Cavalry returned here. News received of capture by Buller of many prisoners, ammunition and wagons, and cattle, and of similar captures by Methuen. 1 Company on outpost.

October 6th.—Rustenburg. Orders received for the Volunteer Company to be sent to Pretoria, *en route* for England. 1 Company on outpost.

October 7th.—Rustenburg. In the afternoon Methuen's Division came in and camped close to the town; thus the West Yorkshires and the 1st Battalion 5th Fusiliers met again for the second time on service. 1 Company on outpost duty.

October 8th.—Rustenburg. Nothing worthy of note.

October 9th.—Rustenburg. Ditto.   2 Companies on outpost.

October 10th.—Rustenburg. Methuen's Division left early in the morning for Magato's Nek. Volunteer Company with Convoy for Pretoria.

October 11th.—Rustenburg. Usual Camp routine.

October 12th.—Rustenburg. Do.

October 13th.—Rustenburg. Sports and Race Meeting was held in the afternoon, attended by the inhabitants of the town.

October 14th.—Rustenburg. Sunday. No Church Parade, owing to high wind.

October 15th.—Rustenburg. E, F, and G Companies under Major Heigham, with 2 Elswick Guns, and 1 Company Argyll and Sutherland Highlanders, the whole under Major Young, R.A., left to hold a small position some 13 miles on the Pretoria road, and to burn out the neighbouring farms.

October 16th.—Rustenburg. Usual Camp routine.

October 17th.—Rustenburg. Convoy arrived from Pretoria.

October 18th.—Rustenburg. Received orders to prepare a draft for India.

October 19th.—Rustenburg. Major Watts with A and B Companies started early in the morning to relieve 2 Companies of the Argyll and Sutherland Highlanders, who were holding Oliphant's Nek. They remain there a week.

About mid-day Major Heigham with E, F, and G Companies returned to Camp, a few prisoners being brought in, and a few wagons burnt. Usual outpost.

October 20th.—Rustenburg. C, D, and H Companies under Major Heigham, with 2 Guns and some M.I., left early in the morning to escort empty Convoy back to Pretoria and to bring a full one out.

News received that Steyn, with 150 burghers, has left Warmbaths, and is trying to work his way down to the Orange River Colony.

October 21st.—Rustenburg. Sunday Church Parade. Machine Gun sent under escort to join Major Watts at Oliphant's Nek. Shortly after mid-day F and 2 Companies of the Argyll and Sutherland Highlanders and 2 Guns left Camp in the direction of Bosh-Hoek. Shortly after they had gone General Broadwood's Force came in, and, after halting for about one hour, followed after them.

October 22nd.—Rustenburg. Broadwood's Force and the Argyll and Sutherland Highlanders and F Company returned about 4 p.m. They had been about 15 miles out, but beyond blowing up a wagon load of ammunition, nothing worthy of note occurred.

October 23rd.—Rustenburg. F Company with 2 Companies Argyll and Sutherland Highlanders and 2 Guns proceeded to Bosh-Hoek at 7-30 a.m. (about 15 miles). Camp was moved at 3 p.m. on to higher ground to a much healthier and more shady place.

Thunderstorms of frequent occurrence, evidently the commencement of the rainy season.

October 24th.—Rustenburg. Broadwood's Force and 2 Companies of the King's Own Yorkshire Light Infantry (who had come in with a Convoy) left about 3 p.m. for Bosh-Hoek. Battalion busily engaged in entrenching.

October 25th.—Rustenburg. Nothing to note.

October 26th.—Rustenburg. C, D, and H Companies under Major Heigham returned about 11 a.m. with Convoy. English Mail arrived. 2 Companies of the King's Own Yorkshire Light Infantry, 2 Guns Royal Horse Artillery, and 1 Squadron 10th Hussars also came in with the Convoy. Still entrenching.
  Lieut. Gretton admitted to Hospital with dysentery. Rumours of an attack to-morrow morning by the enemy.

October 27th.—Rustenburg. E and G Companies paraded at 2-30 p.m.; proceeded back to Rietfontein, forming part of the escort. Last night at dusk the Adjutant of the Argyll and Sutherland Highlanders was sniped at and hit in the arm whilst putting out the outpost.

October 28th.—Rustenburg. Sunday Church Parade. The usual thunderstorm in the evening.

October 29th.—Rustenburg. General Paget and General Plumer came in in the afternoon, and encamped just outside the town.

October 30th.—Rustenburg. F Company proceeded out in the morning to search neighbouring ridges for a small party of Boers, 40 strong, reported to be there. News received of capture of 2 of De Wet's Guns by Knox and Mounted Infantry.

October 31st.—Rustenburg. Paget's and Plumer's Forces marched early in the morning, leaving ½ Battalion Scots Guards behind them. Usual outpost.

November 1st.—Rustenburg. Heavy firing heard all day other side of Magaliesburg; reported to be Paget engaged. Convoy due in to-morrow.

November 2nd.—Rustenburg. Nothing worthy of note. Owing to bad roads Convoy not expected for some days. Usual outpost.

November 3rd.—Rustenburg. Raining hard all night and day. In the afternoon C and H Companies sent down to bivouac in the Dutch Church, out of the rain.

November 4th.—Rustenburg. Sunday Church Parade. Convoy to come in to-morrow.

November 5th.—Rustenburg. Head of Convoy arrived with E and G Companies. Captain Ingles joined from 1st Battalion. 2 Companies and Regimental Head Quarters paraded at 10 a.m., and proceeded to search neighbouring valleys and hills. Out all day, returning to Camp at 5 p.m., bringing in eight horses. Usual outposts.

November 6th.—Rustenburg. Quiet day in Camp. 2 Officers and 50 Men wanted for Mounted Infantry.

November 7th.—Rustenburg. Major Heigham, with D and F Companies, marched off in the morning to relieve Argyll and Sutherland Highlanders, who were holding Magato's Nek. Major Watts returned from Oliphant's Nek in the afternoon, leaving Lieut. Lowe in command there.

November 8th.—Rustenburg. Major Heigham returned from Magato's Nek, and Major Watts went out and took over command there. In the evening A and B Companies marched in from Oliphant's Nek, having been relieved by the Argyll and Sutherland Highlanders. Usual outposts. General Paget's and General Plumer's Columns arrived.

November 9th.—Rustenburg. A and H Companies marched off at 2-30 a.m., and formed part of escort to Convoy, returning to Rietfontein. At 3-30 p.m. the Mounted Infantry Company, 50 strong, under Lieut. Gretton, marched off with the Convoy, their destination being Pretoria, where 2 Brigades of the Mounted Infantry were being formed. Major Heigham also proceeded to Pretoria to take up Staff appointment under General Alderson of the Mounted Infantry.

November 10th.—Rustenburg. Rev. Wainman left with Convoy for Pretoria. News received of the capture of 8 of De Wet's Guns and 100 men by Knox. General Broadwood's Force arrived during the day and camped outside the town.

November 11th.—Rustenburg. Sunday Church Parade. Generals Paget's and Plumer's Columns marched out again early in the morning.

November 12th.—Rustenburg. A year to-day since the Battalion landed at Durban. General Broadwood's Brigade marched in early morning. News received of small successes all round. Usual outposts.

November 13th.—Rustenburg. D and F Companies relieved by G and E Companies at Magato's Nek.

November 14th.—Rustenburg. Nothing to note.

November 15th.—Rustenburg. Usual Camp routine.

November 16th.—Rustenburg. Lieut. Ross arrived at Maritzburg from England. Outpost as usual.

November 17th.—Rustenburg.

November 18th.—Rustenburg. Sunday Church Parade. Weather now very fine, with occasional thunderstorms in the evening.

November 19th.—Rustenburg. Convoy reported to have started from Rietfontein.

November 20th.—Rustenburg. C and D Companies left in the afternoon to relieve Argyll and Sutherland Highlanders. Head Quarters at Oliphant's Nek. General Broadwood's Column returned with a few prisoners.

November 21st.—Rustenburg. E and G Companies under Major Watts returned from Magato's Nek, having been relieved by the Argyll and Sutherland Highlanders.

November 22nd.—Rustenburg. Partial annular Eclipse of the Sun during the early morning.

November 23rd.—Rustenburg. A year ago to-day since the Battle of Willow Grange. First $\frac{1}{2}$ of Convoy arrived during the day.

November 24th.—Rustenburg. Broadwood's Column marched again in early morning.

November 25th.—Rustenburg. Remaining $\frac{1}{2}$ of Convoy with A and H Companies arrived in early morning. Usual Church Parade. 2nd Lieut. Harrington joined Battalion.

November 26th.—Rustenburg. Nothing worthy of note. Usual Camp routine and usual thunderstorms in the evening.

November 27th.—Rustenburg. Broadwood returned again. G and E Companies relieved C and D Companies at Oliphant's Nek.

November 28th.—Rustenburg. B and F Companies left as escort to Convoy.

November 29th.—Rustenburg. Nothing worthy of note. Usual Camp routine. Broadwood left, taking with him $\frac{1}{2}$ Battalion Argyll and Sutherland Highlanders, and leaving $\frac{1}{2}$ Battalion King's Own Yorkshire Light Infantry, who were tired.

November 30th.—Rustenburg. 2 Companies went out to visit neighbouring farms, and returned to Camp about mid-day.

December 1st.—Rustenburg. Morning spent in making a Rifle Range about one and a-half miles from Camp.

December 2nd.—Rustenburg. Usual Church Parade.

December 3rd.—Rustenburg. At 6 a.m. A Company paraded, and marched six miles to Waterkloof; took roof off farm to make shelter for Men, and returned to Camp about 1 p.m. At 1-45 p.m. report received that Convoy had been attacked at Elands Drift, 20 miles from Rustenburg. C and H Companies, with 2 Guns R.F.A. and 20 V.M.R., paraded under command of Major Fry, and proceeded at 3 p.m. to relief of Convoy. As Force marched along the road many Kaffir drivers and conductors were met who had escaped from the Convoy.

At 6 a.m. on the 4th December, it being intensely dark at the time, the advanced guard reported about 100 horses laagered under kopje; as from report of the escaped drivers it appeared that this kopje must be held by Boers. Guns and wagons were packed under cover. C and H Companies, supported by V.M.R., ordered to take kopje at the point of the bayonet. As H Company approached the foot of the kopje it was challenged, and discovered that it was held by our own Men under command of Major Wolridge-Gordon, Argyll and Sutherland Highlanders. Force holding kopje consisted of ½ B Company under Lieut. Lowe, 20 details King's Own Yorkshire Light Infantry, 2 Guns R.F.A., and 10 Men of V.M.R. The Relieving Force at once settled to work to build sangars and defences round remaining wagons (6 of them), which were all that remained of 120 wagons in the Convoy. This work was continued till daylight, when Men had breakfast, and then ½ H Company were ordered to take kopje on side of road, which commanded position, and on which ½ B Company, after a gallant defence, had been captured the previous day.

Search parties were sent out for wounded and any straying oxen and mules; these were fired on by small parties of Boers, who were driven off. Rain had commenced about midnight, and continued almost continuously for 42 hours. About 8 a.m. General Broadwood's Cavalry Brigade arrived from west, and Captain Arbuthnot with some Mounted Infantry arrived from Rietfontein. Under their cover, Ambulances were sent out to spruit, where rear guard of Convoy had fought.

By the afternoon all killed and wounded had been brought in. Total casualties, 18 killed and 24 wounded. Lieut. Barlow and 72 Men captured, 3 missing. The Regiment lost 10 killed, 13 wounded, and 3 missing, Lieut. Barlow and 72 Men captured. About 11 a.m. General Broadwood's Cavalry withdrew to Buffel's Poort. At 3 p.m. 2 sections of Convoy, which had been laagered a day's march in rear, passed with 2 Companies Argyll and Sutherland Highlanders as escort. Last wagon passed at 6 p.m., when our Force formed a rear guard. The Battalion arrived in bivouac at 5 a.m., having been all night in drenching rain. At 3 p.m. the Force marched for Oorzaak. Our Force advanced guard; arriving there about 7 a.m., were bivouacked for the night. At 4 a.m., on the 6th, march resumed for Rustenburg, which was reached about 6 p.m., when it was found that Lieut. Barlow and prisoners had already arrived, having been well treated by the Boers. Estimate in strength of Boers 900, original strength of escort to captured Convoy, 2 Guns Royal Horse Artillery, 2 Companies West Yorkshires (140 Rifles), and 20 V.M.R.

December 7th.—Rustenburg. Refitting in Camp. Court of Enquiry held on Lieut. Barlow and Sergt. Cooley, who commanded 2 parties which were captured. Court honourably acquitted them of all blame, and added a rider expressing admiration of the splendid defence made and good judgment shown by Lieut. Barlow, these parties having held out, though surrounded in an unprepared position, from 5 a.m. to 7 p.m. They only surrendered when last cartridge was expended. Boers assault on kopjes, which held out to the end, was of a most determined nature, pushing attack through scrub and rock to within 50 paces of Guns.

December 8th.—Rustenburg. Major Watts, A Company, and 2 Guns Royal Field Artillery left to reinforce Oliphant's Nek. A good many Boers in the neighbourhood.

December 9th.—Rustenburg. C and D Companies left with 2 Companies Argyll and Sutherland Highlanders and 2 Guns to escort empty Convoy to Rietfontein. Usual Church Parade.

December 10th.—Rustenburg. Rumours of an intended attack on Rustenburg. A good many Boers reported not far off.

December 11th.—Rustenburg. Boers reported to be massing to the numbers of about 4,000 with Guns in our neighbourhood.

December 12th.—Rustenburg. Last night enemy occupied Magato's Pass, which we had to evacuate after the capture of the Convoy.

December 13th.—Rustenburg. Clements attacked by the enemy early in the morning. Lyddite seen bursting some 25 miles off; result not yet known.

December 14th.—Rustenburg. Clements was attacked by 2,000 men under Buyers, and 1,000 men under De la Rey. Heavy casualties on both sides. Botha reported to be coming south from Waterburg. Convoy detained at Riefontein for safety. Broadwood, with Cavalry and $\frac{1}{2}$ Battalion King's Own Yorkshire Light Infantry, arrived in the evening.

B Company under Lieut. Lowe marched at 4 p.m. to reinforce Oliphant's Nek. Garrison there at present consists of 2 Guns Royal Field Artillery, 4 Companies and Machine Gun of West Yorkshire Regiment, the whole under command of Major Watts. 2 Companies, F and H, left at Head Quarters. One of our outpost Companies relieved by King's Own Yorkshire Light Infantry.

December 15th.—Rustenburg. Anniversary of the Battle of Colenso. Early in the morning the C.O. went out to inspect the defences of Oliphant's Nek, and, as it turned out, to take over Command there, as an attack was reported imminent. Lieut. Crossman was left at Head Quarters in charge of F and H Companies.

December 16th.—Oliphant's Nek. The Garrison (2 Guns R.F.A., 4 Companies West Yorkshires, and Maxim) stood to arms at 3 a.m., but nothing unusual occurred. In the morning C.O. ordered to return to Rustenburg, as 8 Officers and nearly 300 Men of the 2nd Battalion Northumberland Fusiliers had been sent there, released prisoners of war from Clements' Force, and had been attached to the Regiment for re-organization. Usual Church Parade at Rustenburg in the morning. Boers reported to be laagered at Bokfontein and Sandfontein.

December 17th.—Rustenburg. Battalion stood to arms and occupied defences at 2-45 a.m. Nothing unusual occurred. Casualties on both sides in Clements' fight very heavy.

December 19th.—Rustenburg. Battalion stood to arms and manned defences at 3-15 a.m. Nothing unusual occurred. Three more days' rations sent out to Oliphant's Nek. Boers still reported to be in their old langers. Started to rain very heavily in the afternoon, and continued all night.

December 20th.—Rustenburg. Stood to arms as usual at 3-15 a.m. Still raining hard, and continued all day. Broadwood left in the afternoon.

December 21st.—Rustenburg. Stood to arms at 3-15 a.m. Heavy showers of rain during the day. Received news that French routed Boers on 19th inst., killing and wounding about 50. Heavy shelling heard in the morning and afternoon in the south-east direction.

Paget, French, Clements, and Broadwood engaged in big movement.

December 22nd.—Rustenburg. The released prisoners of the 5th Fusiliers left us to rejoin Clements, who had returned to Waterkloof with 1,200 M.I., 1,500 Infantry. Duties coming very heavy at present, as out of 2 Companies at Head Quarters one is on outpost, and the other one inlying picquet.

December 23rd.—Rustenburg. Usual Church Parade. Nothing worthy of note.

December 24th.—Rustenburg. Nothing worthy of note.

December 25th.—Rustenburg. Xmas Day Church Parade in the morning.

December 26th.—Rustenburg. Usual Camp routine. Nothing worthy of note.

December 27th.—Rustenburg. A, B, C, and G Companies with Machine Gun, under Major Watts, arrived in the middle of the day from Oliphant's Nek, having been relieved by Argyll and and Sutherland Highlanders.

December 28th.—Rustenburg. Nothing worthy of note.

December 29th.—Rustenburg. Clements with Convoy at Wolhuters Kop.

December 30th.—Rustenburg. Sunday Church Parade. Stood to arms at 3 a.m. Boers reported hastening into neighbourhood. 1 Company on outpost, and an additional Company in support.

December 31st.—Rustenburg. Battalion stood to arms at 3 a.m. Nothing unusual occurred. Convoy still at Wolhuters Kop.

1901.

January 1st.—Rustenburg. Battalion stood to arms at 3 a.m. Clements still at Wolhuter's Kop.

January 2nd.—Rietfontein. Battalion stood to arms as usual at 3 a.m. Nothing worthy of note.

January 3rd.—Rietfontein. Only inlying picquet stood to arms this morning. Convoy with Clements reached Elands Spruit. Received wire stating that Captain Bartrum, Bandmaster Finigan, and 143 Men have left Maritzburg for Pretoria, to join the Battalion Head Quarters.

January 4th.—Rustenburg. Convoy at Buffel's Hoek. Nothing else worthy of note.

January 5th.—Rustenburg. Convoy remained all day at Buffel's Hoek. Shelling heard all the morning from the south of Elands Nek.

January 6th.—Rustenburg. Sunday Church Parade as usual. At 2 a.m. H Company under Lieut. Crossman, with a few M.I., proceeded to a drift east of Krondal to hold it until the Convoy passed. Head of Convoy at Krondal this morning. First half of the Convoy arrived in the evening with the English Mail.

January 7th.—Rustenburg. First half of Convoy left on its return journey : the second half arrived with Capt. Bartrum and a Draft of 134 Recruits, many of whom have not fired a Recruits' Course of Musketry.

January 8th.—Last half of Convoy left for Rietfontein. A very wet night. Cavalry details left for Pretoria, so an extra Company was placed on outpost, making 3 altogether.

January 9th.—Rustenburg. H Company under Lieut. Crossman returned to Camp, without incident. C and E Companies still with Clements, holding road whilst next Convoy comes in.

January 10th.—Rustenburg. Received news of the simultaneous attack on Helvitia, Pan, and Belfast by night. Enemy driven off with loss. Stringent proclamation issued by Lord Kitchener in the taking of prisoners and the abuse of the white flag.

January 11th.—Rustenburg. A and E Companies under Major Watts paraded at 3-10 a.m., and went out in support of V.M.R., who were going to bring cattle from Magato's Stadt.

January 12th.—Rustenburg. Nothing to note.

January 13th.—Rustenburg. Church Parade. Sunday.

January 14th.—Rustenburg. First half of Convoy arrived with Mail in afternoon. H Company under Lieut. Crossman went out with the V.M.R. to bring in Boer families, not returning to Camp till after dark. Received orders to return with Convoy to Pretoria.

January 15th.—Rustenburg. Second half of Convoy arrived. Battalion marches to-morrow.

January 16th.—Rustenburg. Battalion paraded at 3 a.m., and marched to Oorzak (eight miles), 2nd Lieut. Lyster being left behind as Provost Marshal of Rustenburg. Major Watts with F and B Companies were left near Krondal to bring in the rear of the Convoy. Bivouacked for the night.

January 17th.—Oorzak was left at 2-30 a.m., Buffel's Poort, where General Clements was encamped, being reached about 7-30 a.m. Here C and D Companies rejoined the Battalion after an absence of six weeks, and a long halt was made until 3-0 p.m., when Battalion marched to Elands Kraal and bivouacked for the night (15 miles).

January 18th.—Elands Kraal was left at 4 a.m., and the Battalion marched to Bokfontein, which was reached about 7-30 a.m., and where it was intended to bivouac for the night. but about 5 p.m. a sudden order was received for the Battalion to march to Rietfontein, which was reached after a very dusty march at 10-30 p.m. Bivouacked for the night.

January 19th.—Rietfontein was left at 3 a.m. in a tremendous thunderstorm, which did not cease until 8 a.m. Everyone was drenched to the skin and the roads extremely heavy for walking. Pretoria was reached about 4 p.m., and the Battalion went to the Station rest Camp for the night. F and B Companies arrived about 7 p.m.

January 20th.—Pretoria. G Company entrained for Wonderfontein at 3-40 a.m., D Company at 4 a.m., A and B Companies under Major Watts at 11 a.m., and the remainder of the Battalion Head Quarters at noon. The Regiment is to be in a Brigade under Colonel Spens of the K.S.L.I., in General Smith-Dorrien's Division, to operate in the country south of Belfast.

Head Quarter's train arrived at Balmoral about 6-30 p.m., where a halt was made for the night.

January 21st.—Balmoral. Train left about 7 a.m. After proceeding about six miles, just before reaching Brugspruit, a mine, evidently badly laid, exploded under the second engine, luckily without doing any damage to the train, and at the same time a few Boers opened fire on the train, which continued on its way. The fire was at once returned; no casualties, several Men having very narrow escapes. Middleburg was reached safely about 2 a.m., where the remainder of the Battalion had detrained, with the exception of F Company, which had been sent on to Wonderfontein by train with a Howitzer.

News received of the Queen's serious illness.

January 22nd.—Middleburg. Battalion, with 3 Squadrons of the 18th Hussars, left at 12-50 p.m. with Convoy for Pan, which was reached without incident about 6 p.m., after an easy march of about 13 miles.

Bivouacked for the night.

January 23rd.—Pan. Battalion, with Convoy and Hussars, marched at 5-30 a.m. for Wonderfontein, which was reached about 3 p.m. A few Boer scouts were seen on the way, who were driven off by the Cavalry and a Pom-pom at Wonderfontein. Joined our new Brigade, consisting of 1st Suffolk Regiment, 2nd West Yorkshire Regiment, 1st East Surrey Regiment, and 1st Cameron Highlanders, under Colonel Spens, K.S.L.I.

January 24th.—Wonderfontein. Quiet day in Camp, preparing for to-morrow's move.

News received of the Queen's death. About mid-day a salute of about 21 Guns was fired in honour of the Prince of Wales's accession.

49

G and F Companies went out at 7-30 a.m. to support Cavalry, who collected families from the farms around; they returned to Camp about 2 p.m.

January 25th.—Wonderfontein was left at 5-15 a.m., Battalion forming part of the main body. The Force marched in a southerly direction, the rear and flank guards being engaged *en route* with small parties of the enemy. On reaching Twyfelaar, a distance of 18 miles, the Boers took up position on some small kopjes and woods, which they held till nightfall. The Regiment did not come into action. Our casualties were Major Lloyd (of the Suffolks) killed, and 15 Men wounded. Boers admitted loss of one killed and four wounded. Very heavy thunderstorm about dusk, one man of the Suffolks being killed by lightning. Bivouacked for the night.

January 26th.—Twyfelaar was left at 5 a.m., Battalion forming advanced guard. Cavalry engaged all the way with small parties of the enemy. On reaching hills around Carolina, which were thought to be fairly strongly held, a long halt was made to allow the baggage to close up; meanwhile the 5-inch Guns bombarded the position and the Mounted Troops commenced to work round the Boers' left. After waiting some time the Battalion advanced, supported by the Essex on our right. The Boers, however, retired, and the town was entered without opposition. Bivouacked at the east end of the town. A wet evening, which cleared up about 1 o'clock. Horse and six mules died from horse sickness.

January 27th.—Carolina. Sunday. At 9-30 a.m. the Force marched from Carolina to Twyfelaar, the West Yorkshire Regiment with most of the Mounted Troops forming the rear guard. About one hour after starting heavy rain and hailstones commenced, which lasted several hours. After crossing Bushman's Spruit the Boers appeared in considerable numbers, and commenced harassing rear guard. At dusk they brought 2 Pom-poms and 1 High-velocity 12-pounder into action. About 7 p.m. the Boers retired, and our Force moved on to bivouac on Komati River.

CASUALTIES.

No. 5385 Pte. Nelson (severely wounded).
Duffledar Selor (killed).
2 Mules (killed).

January 28th.—At 6 a.m. Force marched to Klipfontein, about eight miles, where main body bivouacked for the night. The Cameron Highlanders with some of the Mounted Troops proceeded in charge of Convoy to Wonderfontein. Boers slightly harassed the march.

January 29th.—Remained at Klipfontein all day, but orders to move to Twyfelaar at 4 p.m., which were cancelled. Captain Fisher and Lieut. Lowe joined Battalion coming out from Wonderfontein with Convoy, which arrived that evening. Cavalry Patrol went out in the morning and were sniped by Boers, whereupon 2 Field

Guns went out, D Company acting as escort; there was a little firing and the sniping ceased.

January 30th.—Battalion moved at 9-30 a.m. as advanced guard to Force, which went back to Wonderfontein. Heavy thunderstorm in the afternoon.

January 31st.—Still at Wonderfontein. Got the tents of the Essex, who moved to Pretoria. The Drums played in the evening.

February 1st.—Remained at Wonderfontein. H Company proceeded to Middleburg to escort back remounts.

February 2nd.—Still at Wonderfontein, busy getting ready for tomorrow's move.

February 3rd.—Force moved to Twyfelaar. Battalion moved as rear guard to Force. March continued without interruption, not a shot fired all day. Battalion started at 5-45 a.m., and reached bivouac across Twyfelaar Drift at 3-30 p.m. A trying march, as the day was extremely hot (18 miles' march).

February 4th.—Battalion moved off at 5-30 a.m. as 2nd Regiment. March was slow and tiring on account of boggy condition of ground and several spruits. The Convoy delayed the Column because of the frequent halts that were necessary to allow it to close up. There was no firing. We reached Camp at 3-30 p.m.; name of the place Outskend.

February 5th.—Battalion moved off at 4 a.m. as advanced guard to Force, which proceeded to Lake Chrissie; there was a little sniping, and the Boers opened fire with a Pom-pom on the rear guard, doing no damage. As the Force neared Lake Chrissie we saw a large number of Boer wagons trekking in a south-easterly direction. All available Mounted Troops with 2 Field Guns were sent in pursuit, and the 5-inch Gun was hurried up and fired some shots, all of which fell short. The Mounted Troops returned to Camp shortly after the Battalion settled down, which was about 2-30 p.m., having had no success. The Boers are supposed to have gone to Amsterdam.

February 6th.—At 2-55 a.m. a determined attack was made by the Boers on our Camp, the main attack being delivered on the outpost line held by the West Yorkshire Regiment. The attack lasted until 4-10 a.m., when the Boers retired. The Men behaved with great coolness and steadiness, and made a very determined stand.

The following order was issued the same evening by Major-General Smith-Dorrien:—

"The G.O.C. compliments most highly the steadiness of all Infantry Battalions in the outpost line during the heavy attack last night. The conduct of the West Yorkshires, on whom the brunt of the battle fell, was especially fine, and their heavy losses are deplored. The casualties were very heavy owing to the Boers getting through two picquets having followed up a mob of 200 stampeded cavalry horses; these two picquets were practically wiped out."

Our casualties were:—

KILLED.

Lieut. Cantor.	Private Myers, J.
Sergeant Greensmith.	„ Stokes, H.
Corporal Taylor, H.	„ Dyson, H.
„ Deglow, E.	„ Hawksley, H.
Private Walker, R.	„ Fletcher, W.
„ Knight, B.	„ Crosby, A.
„ Stead, W.	„ Middleton, A.
„ Hurton, I.	„ Snead, J.
„ Lindley, J.	„ Onslow, J.
„ Sear, F.	„ Clarkson, H.

WOUNDED.

Cr.-Sergeant Lyons.	Private Marshall, T.
„ Busher.	„ Smith, J.
Sergeant Woodhouse, F.	„ Globe, A.
„ Traynor, W.	„ Paul, W.
„ Warwick, W.	„ Cotter, T.
„ Farrar, B.	„ Clark, T.
Lce.-Corporal Bell, J.	„ Clark, J. C.
Private Wright, W.	„ Walker, F.
„ Freen, H.	„ Garner, A.
„ Devine, J.	„ Snowdon, F.
„ Cox, J.	„ Bourne, W.
„ Lewington, J.	„ Amos, B.
„ Holland, F.	„ Selby, A.
„ Smith, J.	„ Lawrence, E.
„ Hayes, J.	

Six Boers were found in front of our lines, and 27 casualties have been seen; there were probably more. Our casualties would have been much heavier but for the outpost being entrenched, which is the usual custom of the Battalion.

February 7th.—Force remained stationary at Lake Chrissie. ½ Battalion paraded under Major Watts, and went out to meet Colonel Campbell's Column, which arrived at Lake Chrissie about 1-30 p.m. Colonel Campbell's Column reached Camp in the evening, having with it the 14th M.I. under Major Heigham. There was heavy rain during the day.

February 8th.—Force remained at Lake Chrissie. Pouring with rain nearly all day. Major Heigham paid us a visit, having come in the evening before with Alderson's Force.

February 9th.—Force moved to Lillieborn. Battalion started at 5-35 a.m. as rear guard to the Force. March was very slow on account of the condition of the ground after yesterday's rain. Many wagons got stuck, and had to be helped on by different

Companies. Colonel Henry with his Mounted Men had a very successful day, capturing 50 Boer wagons and 400 oxen, also 4,000 sheep. One Boer killed and three wounded; 20 Boers taken prisoners. Colonel Campbell's Column followed us in rear for a short time, then cut off on our right flank in an easterly direction. Our Force at present moving in an easterly direction.

February 10th.—Battalion started at 2 p.m. as leading Battalion of the main body. Most of the morning was employed at fatigues, getting the wagons over the drift, Umpilusi River. The march was a short one, only being about four or five miles. In the evening volunteers were called for to kill sheep, the Men being allowed a penny a head for each sheep killed. A good many volunteered. The name of the place was Warburton.

February 11th.—Battalion started at 8-30 a.m. as advanced guard to Force, which moved to Craigilia. The early part of the morning was employed in killing sheep, each Battalion supplying 200 Men. About 15,000 were slaughtered, the remainder being driven to our next Camp. Battalion arrived in Camp about 3-30 p.m.

Force had to camp this side of drift owing to the difficulty in crossing. The Cameron Highlanders were ordered to go across, and most of them had to swim.

February 12th.—Battalion moved across the drift at 4 p.m., being the last to go over. ½ Battalion under Major Watts did outpost on the same side as the Battalion had been camped on. About 3,000 more sheep were captured by the Mounted Troops. We were on fatigue most of the day at the drift.

February 13th.—Force moved from Craigilia to Weston. Battalion formed rear guard to Force. There was a little sniping, no damage being done. Several more horses and cattle were captured. Battalion reached Camp about 6 p.m. (distance of march 18 miles).

February 14th.—Battalion paraded about 6-15 p.m. and with Suffolk Regiment. Most of Mounted Troops and some Guns went in a southerly direction by Lichfield Store, where some Boers were found, and kept up sniping for some time. They were eventually dislodged, and the Force continued its march towards Amsterdam, the Suffolks, with a Section of Royal Artillery and some Mounted Infantry, being left at the Store. When the Regiment reached Twepoort, they were left with a Section of Royal Artillery and some Mounted Infantry at another post, the remainder of the Troops going on to Amsterdam, about six miles further on. Our casualties were two Officers Mounted Infantry wounded, and one Man. March about 12 miles. The remainder of the Convoy went straight to Amsterdam, escorted by the Camerons and rest of Mounted Troops with Guns.

February 15th.—Battalion remained at Twepoort. About mid-day orders came that 150 Boers with 1 Gun were moving across our front, south of Amsterdam. 3 Companies, 2 Guns, and all available Mounted Troops went out immediately to endeavour to intercept them. The whole Force was under Major Fry. There was a little sniping in front at the Mounted Infantry, and, on the Guns being brought into action, the enemy cleared. The Mounted Troops went a long distance to the front, the remaining Troops supporting, but no signs of the force reported could be seen.

Companies in Camp were busy all day entrenching themselves.

February 16th.—Battalion still at Twepoort. The Imperial Light Horse under Colonel Mackenzie arrived the evening before, and joined our Force at Twepoort. Rained all day and all night.

February 17th.—Still at Twepoort. Rained all day and night.

February 18th.—Still at Twepoort. Still raining.

February 19th.—Battalion still at Twepoort. Weather cleared at 7 a.m., after raining all night. ½ Battalion moved to Lichfield to take over the Suffolks' post, the latter going out as one of the Columns to round up Boers and cattle on the Swaziland Border. 2 Companies of ours also went out with a 5-inch Gun with a different Column, all taking part in the same movement, 2 Companies of the Camerons coming over from Amsterdam to take over some of our posts. Columns did not return till late, but had a successful day capturing a lot of cattle, bringing in one prisoner, killing one of the enemy, and wounding one. Our casualties, nil.

February 20th.—The Battalion moved from Twepoort to Amsterdam, the Suffolks also moving from Lichfield to Amsterdam. The whole Force was to have moved to Wolven Kop to-morrow, but, owing to heavy rains, was unable to go, the river having risen four feet since last night. Rained incessantly all day and night.

February 21st.—Rained all day and night. Battalion on half rations owing to the Convoy under Colonel Burne-Murdock being delayed through heavy rains and swollen rivers. Still at Amsterdam.

February 22nd.—Rained all day and night. Force remained on small rations. Fatigue parties sent out to collect all mealies and any eatable matter. No news of Convoy. Still at Amsterdam.

February 23rd.—Still at Amsterdam. The weather improved a bit, much of the day being fine. Parties still going out for mealies.

February 24th.—Rained most of the night before, and cleared up about 9 a.m. Companies sent to farms about to collect mealies. Boers fired on one party of 5th Lancers approaching farm, killing one Man and wounding two.

February 25th.—Force moved from Amsterdam to Sterkfontein, about five miles, Battalion forming advanced guard. Nothing startling occurred. Force unable to get across river at present.

February 26th.—Force moved from Sterkfontein to Wolven Kop, Battalion forming rear guard to Force. March about seven miles.

There was a little sniping. No casualties. It was a long day owing to the Compies River, which had to be crossed, and a couple of drifts.

February 27th.—Force moved from Wolven Kop to Derby, about 11 miles. Battalion was leading Battalion of main body. Alderson's Column was seen camped about three miles away. Major Heigham with Lieuts. Gretton and Fryer paid us a visit on the march. Force still living on the country. No signs of Convoy.

February 28th.—Force remained at Derby. Most of Mounted Troops left Camp to try and capture a Boer Convoy which was sighted. Two Boers surrendered during the morning. No sign of Convoy.

March 1st.—Force remained at Derby. 1 Company of Regiment escorted empty wagons of Convoy, which arrived in the morning, back to Piet Retief; only six wagons came in, not having much on them ; most of the Convoy still on the other side of the Assagai River. Things were slung across ; a bridge was constructed.

March 2nd.—Still at Derby. Nothing exciting happened. Had some rain during the day. Heard in the evening that Colonel Henry had captured the Convoy which he went in pursuit of, with 56 prisoners, and that Commandant Inglebrecht had gone into Piet Retief to surrender with 30 more ; there were also a lot of cattle and sheep taken.

March 3rd.—Remained at Derby. 2 Companies under Major Watts went out with a Force commanded by Colonel King, 5th Lancers, to destroy a mill about seven miles from our Camp. They succeeded in their purpose, but a Force of the Lancers, which was supposed to be keeping a look out on a kopje, was attacked by the Boers (who numbered eight), and had four Men wounded and one taken prisoner.

Five or six wagons continued coming in daily from Piet Retief. Force still on half rations.

March 4th.—Remainder of wagons which Colonel Henry captured came into Camp, the whole numbering 26. Arrangements were made for getting a Canteen out for the Men from Volksrust.

March 5th.—Wretched morning ; thick mist, accompanied by rain, which lasted all day. Owing to the mist a Convoy of empty wagons, Boer families, and cattle, which was to have gone into Piet Retief, was postponed.

March 6th.—Rained all night. Mist cleared slightly, enough to enable the Convoy to proceed to Piet Retief, C and D Companies under Captain Carey forming escort. Rained, off and on, all day. Force still at Derby.

March 7th.—Miserable night and rained all day. C and D Companies returned from Piet Retief mid-day. They met the 2nd Devons there, who had escorted Convoy from Volksrust. No news, owing to wire being cut.

March 8th.—Cleared up in the morning after raining all night, but commenced raining about 10 a.m. and continued all day and night. No further news.

March 9th.—Cleared up in the morning and remained fine all day. Communication was got up between Volksrust and ourselves by means of heliograph, there being an intermediate station at Spitz Kop. One of our Men discovered some Boer Martini Ammunition in a spruit while washing; there were about 350 rounds.

March 10th, 11th, 12th, 13th, and 14th.—Force remained at Derby. Rained incessantly day and night.

March 15th.—Force moved from Derby to Piet Retief, Battalion as advanced guard. Nothing occurred of any note. Arrived at Piet Retief. Battalion was split up into two $\frac{1}{2}$ Battalions—one under Major Watts, with A, B, C, and E Companies holding one hill, the other, with Head Quarters, holding another hill. Camping grounds very dirty and smelly, General French's Troops having left same ground in the morning.

March 16th.—Piet Retief. Nothing worthy of note occurred.

March 17th.—Piet Retief. A new scheme of outposts were devised. The Battalion was out all day making forts, outpost scheme being to have a ring of forts on high hills round the town, and an inner line of defence close to and round the town, each fort to be held by a Company or a $\frac{1}{2}$ Company according to its size.

March 18th, 19th, and 20th.—Battalion still holding defences.

March 21st.—Convoy of rations arrived from Volksrust. No stores. Next Convoy expected 25th. A Mail also expected by it.

March 22nd.—Battalion moved from hill above the town to the latter. We have two houses—one for Officers' Mess, other for Sergeants—and recreation and reading rooms. F and G Companies manned the forts.

March 23rd.—B and G Companies, with 50 Mounted Infantry and 2 Field Guns, proceeded under command of Major Watts to a place called Normandie, about 15 miles from here; they are there to form and entrench Camp for the purpose of guarding the telegraph wires. Remainder of Battalion busy entrenching.

March 24th.—Church Parade in the morning in the Dutch Church. Most of Battalion busy entrenching.

March 25th.—Convoy commenced coming in in the morning; otherwise nothing exciting occurred.

March 26th.—Remainder of Convoy came in, bringing our Mails from Wonderfontein. Battalion had not had a Mail since the beginning of January. Mails also went out with returning Convoy.
  No mess stores arrived, so we are still on half rations.

March 27th, 28th, and 29th.—Battalion still improving trenches. On the 29th, D and E Companies relieved C and F Companies at the fort. There was a thunderstorm in the afternoon of the 29th, very heavy rain.

March 30th and 31st.—Still at Piet Retief.

April 1st and 2nd.—Nothing to record.

April 3rd.—Convoy arrived, bringing chiefly oats. Major Yale came with it, having come out from home. 2nd Lieut. Porch came down from fort with fever, and was sent to Hospital, 2nd Lieut. Harrington taking over D Company.

April 4th.—H Company relieved A Company at fort, nothing otherwise taking place.

April 5th.—Good Friday. Had Church Parade. E Company relieved D Company at fort (Redhill), Captain Bartrum taking over charge of Redhill Fort.

April 6th and 7th.—Easter Church Parade in the morning in the Dutch Church.

April 8th and 9th.—Nothing to note.

April 10th.—F Company relieved H Company at the fort. Convoy commenced coming in on the morning. The following Officers, N.C.O.'s, and Men have been mentioned from time to time in Despatches, and appeared in the *London Gazette* on February 8th, 1901 :—

> "1939 Sergeant G. Ford, Monte Christo, 19th February, 1900. When both Company Officers were shot, he commanded his Company with cool judgment and courage."

Sir Redvers Buller's Despatch of the 30th March, 1900 :—

> "1750 Sergeant F. H. Poplar. (Killed in action 27th February, 1900.) Throughout operations 14th to 27th he always showed conspicuous coolness and courage."
>
> "4778 Private J. Moran, 21st February, 1900. Volunteered to carry back a message from Lieut. Boyall under very heavy fire, and was wounded whilst doing so."
>
> "4560 Private H. Goodyear, 24th January, 1900. Spion Kop. Conspicuous gallantry as signaller, in signalling all day under very heavy fire."

Sir Redvers Buller's Despatch, 30th March, 1900 :—

> "Major Fry, Major H. E. Watts, Captain J. H. Berney (killed), Lieut. and Act. Adjt. L. H. Spry, Lieut. H. S. Pennel, V.C., 2nd Derby Regiment (attached), Lieut. O. H. L. Nicholson."

Sir Redvers Buller's Despatch, 1st February, 1900;—

> "Colonel F. W. Kitchener reports that Lieut. A. M. Boyall conducted a patrol to within 500 yards of the Boer trenches to examine ground for an advance. Out of 16 Men he had only one Man killed and two wounded, although exposed all day to the full view of the enemy on open ground and on a grass slope. His conduct showed exceptional coolness and gallantry.
>
> "4788 Private J. Moran. Carried back a message from Lieut. Boyall under very heavy fire, and was wounded."

"2924 Private Powell. Twice carried water to wounded Men lying out in the open under heavy fire."

"Cr.-Sergeant Kingsley. When his Company was unexpectedly caught by a heavy cross fire, which wounded both his Officers, showed coolness and intelligence in withdrawing his Men steadily to cover, and gallantry in bringing his Captain under cover when mortally wounded. His case is an exceptional one, worthy of recommendation for the Medal for Distinguished Conduct."

Sir Redvers Buller's Despatch, 19th June, 1900. The following names are mentioned by Commanders as having performed good services in addition to those previously mentioned:—

2ND BATTALION WEST YORKSHIRE REGIMENT.

Major W. Fry. Commanding.
Major H. E. Watts.
3325 Sergeant J. Walmsley.
5054 Private T. Dodd.

Sir Redvers Buller's Despatch, 9th November, 1900:—

" The 2nd Battalion West Yorkshire Regiment was, after the promotion of Colonel Kitchener, commanded by Major Fry, who proved himself a most capable Commander, and the Regiment well maintained its high character.

The following Officers and N.C.O.'s merit special mention :—

Major H. E. Watts.
Captain C. E. Wood, 1st Volunteer Battalion.
Lieut. S. G. Francis (an excellent transport Officer).
2nd Lieut. C. J. H. Lyster.
No. 3147 Sergeant A. E. Bridle.
No. 721 1st Class Army Sergeant H. Southern.
No. 3325 Sergeant J. Walmsley (who distinguished himself in charge of the Maxims of the Battalion).
No. 2430 Corporal P. Conroy (who proved himself a most gallant and trustworthy soldier)."

Large Convoy of about 500 wagons arrived from Volksrust, bringing supplies of all sorts for the Force.

The following Officers arrived with the Convoy :—Captain and Adjutant A. C. Daly (from sick leave home); Lieut. A. M. Boyall from Hospital, Wonderfontein ; 2nd Lieut. E. F. Welchman, to join of first appointment.

April 11th.—B and G Companies under Major Watts rejoined Head Quarters from Jagt Drift, where they had been on detachment.

April 12th.—Nothing to record. Empty Convoy started to return to Volksrust. The following Officers left the Battalion with Convoy :—Captain J. S. Bartrum, sick list, and to go eventually to 1st Battalion ; 2nd Lieut. E. A. Porch, sick list ; 2nd Lieut. C. L. Barlow, transferred to 1st Battalion ; Civil Surgeon Collier, in medical charge of Battalion, also left *en route* for England, his place being taken by Civil Surgeon Dyer.

April 13th.—Received orders in the morning to march in the afternoon. Battalion paraded at 2 p.m., and marched out about two miles north of Piet Retief, where we camped. The Supply Column accompanied the Battalion, and was parked for the night under our charge. C and D Companies on picquet. Remainder of the Battalion were in a circle round the Camp, with an interval of about 150 yards between Companies. The remainder of our Column (Major-General Smith-Dorrien's) remained in Piet Retief for the night.

April 14th.—Sunday. Marched at 7-45 a.m. The Battalion forming the advanced guard to the Column. Direction of route, north-north-west, to the Sheld River, about 11 miles. A party of the enemy occupied Van Rogen's Farm, about half a mile south of the river, and opened fire on a patrol of the 6th Dragoon Guards, killing one Man. They then galloped off. The General ordered the farm and buildings and fruit trees, &c., to be destroyed; this was done. A long check occurred at the river, which was crossed by means of a pontoon bridge and a drift. About 100 wagons had to remain on south side of the river for the night, under charge of the Suffolk Regiment. The West Yorkshires and Mounted Troops encamped on north side of the river. E and F Companies were on picquet, G and H in support.

April 15th.—March continued, direction north-west, Battalion acting as rear guard. Marched about 10 miles, reaching Sanbult about 3-30 p.m. A bog delayed the wagons considerably, and we halted for the night. 5th Lancers, 2 Guns 84th Battery Royal Field Artillery, and 1 5-inch Gun remained with us. A and H Companies on outpost, B and G in support. Remainder of Force encamped about five miles ahead on the south side of river. Lieut.-Colonel Campbell's Column encamped about five miles west of our Force.

April 16th.—Did not continue march till 2 p.m., owing to difficulty in getting over bog. Head Quarters and A, B, C, and G Companies moved forward about four miles; the remainder of the Battalion under Major Yale stayed behind with supply wagons at the bog. B and C Companies furnished outposts for Head Quarters.

April 17th.—Head Quarters moved forward about four miles, crossed River Compies and encamped on north bank, about half a mile from river at Glen Elands. A and C Companies on picquet. The other ½ Battalion under Major Yale remained at the drift, covering the crossing.

April 18th.—Marched at 6-15 a.m., Battalion acting as advanced guard. Remainder of Battalion rejoined Head Quarters encamped at Bank Plaats, about 12 miles north-west of Glen Elands. The enemy offered a certain amount of opposition about 1-30 p.m., taking up a position on Bank Kop, a formidable hill directly on our front. The Artillery shelled them, and, covered by their fire, the Battalion advanced on the hill, G and C Companies in support. The other 3 Companies were in rear with the Convoy. The Mounted Troops, with Pom-pom Section under Colonel Henry, worked round the enemy's left flank, whereupon they speedily evacuated their position, coming under the fire of the Pom-pom in their retreat. Three horses were killed by our fire, and two men were seen to fall; a few snipers fired at our leading Companies, but there were no casualties—one horse of the Imperial Light Horse was killed. G Company captured between 500 and 600 sheep on Bank Kop. E and G Companies held the position they had gained during the night. C Company were also on picquet, holding a small hill north-east of Camp. Remainder of Battalion encamped on Bank Plaats, a plateau lying east of Bank Kop, and about 400 feet below the summit occupied by E and G Companies.

April 19th.—Continued march at 6-15 a.m., and reached Roodeval, about eight miles on, at 11-30 a.m. Battalion on advanced guard. Orders were eventually issued to camp there for the night. Several parties of Boers, the largest being about 100, were seen on the hills round about, and were shelled by the 5-inch Gun and the Pom-poms. B, D, and H Companies on outpost.

April 20th.—Battalion acted as rear guard. A, F, C, and E Companies, under Major Yale, moved off at about 9 a.m. to the first drift, about one and a-half miles from Camp, where they remained on fatigue, helping wagons over. Head Quarters and the other 4 Companies remained on the hill, covering the drift and the retirement of the Imperial Light Horse, who had been engaged with the enemy since early morning. A few snipers moved up to within 1,000 yards and engaged us. B and D Companies and the Machine under Sergeant Walmsley fired a good many rounds. 2 Guns Royal Field Artillery were also in action. Our casualties were two Men Imperial Light Horse wounded, and one horse killed. Enemy's loss unknown, but one man was seen to fall from his horse. The last Convoy wagon crossed the drift at about 4 p.m., and the rear guard was then gradually withdrawn. Another drift then had to be crossed about two miles further on, and, as it was impossible to get several of the wagons on, owing to darkness, a laager was formed there for the night under Colonel Mackenzie, Imperial Light Horse. This detached Force consisted of 2 Squadrons Imperial Light Horse, 1 5-inch Gun and 2 Guns Royal Field Artillery, and A, C, D, and E Companies 2nd West Yorkshire Regiment, under Major Yale. As all our baggage had been pushed on to the main Camp, these Companies passed a cold, uncomfortable night, without great coats or blankets. Head Quarters and B, F, G, and H Companies pushed on to the main Camp at Smithfield, about four and a-half miles further on, which was reached at about 8-30 p.m. F and G Companies on outpost.

April 21st.—Sunday. The Force halted for the day, to rest the oxen and baggage and animals. A bright warm day, which gave everyone a chance to get a welcome wash and a change of clothes.

Major Yale and the Companies which had been left behind rejoined Head Quarters. B and H Companies on outpost.

April 22nd.—Marched at 6 a.m. Battalion on advanced guard. The roads were in a good condition, only a few bits of boggy ground being encountered. We were able to make the best march since leaving Piet Retief, covering about 16 miles, direction north-north-west. Halted for the night at Lilyput. The Force encamped around a large pan, the perimeter of the Camp being about two miles. C and D Companies and 1 Section A Company were on outpost, covering a line of about 1,400 yards long on front face of Camp. Communication by heliograph was established with Wonderfontein during the day. The Mounted Troops came in for a certain amount of sniping, and, just before reaching Camp, the enemy opened fire with a Pom-pom. There were no casualties on our side.

Colonel Campbell's Column, which was marching about 10 miles west of, and parallel with, us, was engaged most of the day in what appeared to be a rear-guard action. We heard continuous Artillery fire for many hours, and the enemy were said to have 2 14-pounder Creusot Guns, 1 Howitzer, 1 Pom-pom, and 3 Maxims.

April 23rd.—The Force halted for·the day. A and T Companies on outposts.

April 24th.—Marched about 11 miles in a westerly direction, and encamped at Klipfontein. The Battalion acted as rear guard. A little sniping on the road, but no casualties. B and H Companies on outposts. Had a message from Wonderfontein to the effect that on reaching the line the Battalion was to proceed to Pretoria.

April 25th.—Marched about 7-30 p.m., and marched about 10 miles north-west to Shaap Kraal, where we outspanned to let the rear close up. No sniping. The roads in excellent condition, but water scarce. The Force halted for the night, as the next water supply was nine miles further on, and it was doubtful whether the rear guard would be in by nightfall. C and D Companies on outposts.

April 26th.—Force marched off at 7 a.m. in a northerly direction. Made 17 miles, and halted for the night at Vlakfontein. The Battalion acted as rear guard. A few Boers followed up and sniped. One Officer and one Man of the M.T.'s were slightly wounded, and one horse killed. Our casualties nil. C and F Companies on outposts.

April 27th.—Battalion on advanced guard. ½ Battalion A, B, C, and D Companies under Major Yale moved off at 5-20 a.m. as escort to Ox Supply Park. Remainder of Battalion moved off at 7 a.m. As usual a certain amount of sniping took place on the march, but the Battalion had no casualties. Reached Wonderfontein about 4 p.m. A very trying hot march of about 16 miles. Found that Lieuts. Nicholson, Shuttleworth, and Lupton had gone off with

Major-General Kitchener's Column. Tents were issued, and we made ourselves comfortable. No outposts were furnished by the Battalion. Found Captain Trevor at Wonderfontein, having been posted to the Battalion on the expiration of his five years as Adjutant of the 3rd Battalion.

April 29th.—Received information that we should be proceeding to Pretoria the next day. G Company on outposts. On the breaking up of General Smith-Dorrien's Force, the following orders were issued by him and Colonel Spens, commanding the Infantry Brigade.

FORCE ORDERS No. 4 of 28-4-01.

"It is now over three months since Smith-Dorrien's Force started on the last operations. Never had Troops greater hardships to undergo, and undergone them with greater cheerfulness. Night outposts have been especially heavy, so much that it has been necessary to use the Mounted Troops equally with the Infantry. As the composition of Smith-Dorrien's Force is likely to be changed before it again moves, the Major-General in Command takes this opportunity of thanking all ranks most warmly for the hearty way they have worked for him, and it will give him much pleasure to bring to General-Commander-in-Chief the excellent work done by all units and by individuals. He feels that his promotion to the rank of Major-General, which Lord Kitchener has just announced, is a tribute to the way the Force has worked, and he hopes that many more will reap reward, which they have undoubtedly earned."

BRIGADE ORDER No. 7 of 28-4-01, on the breaking up of Spen's Brigade.

"The Brigadier wishes to thank all ranks of the Brigade for the excellent work they have done during the time he has had the honour to command them. The cheerful spirit shown by all during the period of exceptional hardships has been most noticeable, and in bidding them good-bye the Brigadier wishes them also God-speed. He will always remember with pride his associations with them, and trusts some day to have the honour to meet them again."

April 30th.—A, B, and C Companies, with Commanding Officer, Adjutant, and Quartermaster, entrained at 9 a.m. for Pretoria. Owing to a long and inexplicable delay at Middleburg it was not possible to get beyond Witbank, where a halt was made for the night.

May 1st.—Continued journey, reaching Pretoria without incident about 2-30 p.m. Marched to Arcadia Camp.

May 2nd.—D and E Companies, under Major Watts, arrived about 12-30 p.m., and the remainder of the Battalion arrived about 8-30 p.m., under Major Yale. 2nd Lieut. Grant-Dalton and 2nd Lieut. Wallace joined Battalion.

May 3rd.—D Company, made up to 100 strong (from C Company), paraded under Captain Trevor and 2nd Lieut. Wallace at 7-30 a.m., and proceeded by rail to Eerste Fabrieken to relieve a post of King's Own Scottish Borderers. A and B Companies under Lieuts. Lowe and Lemon paraded at 8 a.m., and proceeded to the outposts to relieve the Northumberland Fusiliers. The second Volunteer Service Company joined the Battalion. E Company, made up to 75 strong (by G Company), paraded at 11-30 a.m. under Lieut. Boyall, and proceeded to the West Fort, also to relieve the Northumberland Fusiliers. Captain Pearson and Lieuts. Ellis, Hirst, and Huffam arrived with Volunteer Service Company Draft.

May 4th.—Head Quarters, consisting of Major Fry (Commanding), Major Yale (2nd in Command), Major Watts, Captain and Adjutant Daly, Lieut. Francis (Transport Officer), and F Company (Lieuts. Riall and Grant-Dalton), paraded at 6 a.m., and moved to Daaspoort, taking over quarters from Northumberland Fusiliers. A Composite Company, consisting of H Company and balance of G and E Companies, under Captain Carey and 2nd Lieut. Welchman, proceeded to Quagga Redoubt, and took over the defences. The Volunteer Service Company took over seven blockhouses in the western outpost line. 51 details of various Companies under Lieut. A. H. Cuthell rejoined Head Quarters from the rest Camp.

May 5th.—Lieut. A. H. Cuthell (on return from sick leave home) and 51 Men of various Companies rejoined the Battalion from Details Camp.

May 6th.—Nothing to record.

May 7th.—Ditto.

May 8th.—Ditto.

May 9th.—A detachment of 86 N.C.O.'s and Men, under Lieut. O. H. L. Nicholson and 2nd Lieuts. Shuttleworth and Lupton, rejoined the Battalion from Belfast. This was the detachment which had been with General Walter Kitchener's Column.

May 10th.—Nothing to record.

May 11th.—2nd Lieut. J. K. Clothier joined the Battalion from England on first appointment, and was posted to E Company.

May 12th.—Sunday Church Parade at 9-15 a.m.

May 13th.—F Company left Head Quarters at Daaspoort at 6 a.m., and relieved E Company at West Fort. E Company relieved 2nd Volunteer Service Company at Daasrand East, who returned to Head Quarters.

May 14th.—H Company under Lieut. Nicholson and Lieut. Shuttleworth, and 15 N.C.O's and Men under 2nd Lieut. Welchman, relieved A and B Companies at Quagga Fort and Johannesburg Road Redoubt. A Company proceeded to Quagga Redoubt for duty, and B Company rejoined Head Quarters for duty at Daaspoort.

May 15th.—25 N.C.O's and Men of C Company proceeded to Eerste Fabrieken by 7 a.m. train to reinforce detachment under command of H. B. Trevor.

May 16th.—Nothing to record.

May 17th.—Ditto.

May 18th.—Ditto.

May 19th.—Sunday Church Parade.

May 20th.—Nothing to record.

May 21st.—Lieut. Riall went to General Elliott's Column as Signalling Officer.

May 22nd.—Nothing to record.

May 23rd.—B Company relieved F Company at West Fort. F Company relieved E Company at Daasrand West. E Company rejoined Head Quarters.

May 24th.—Nothing to record.

May 25th.—Ditto.

May 26th.—Sunday Church Parade at 9 a.m.

May 27th.—Nothing to record.

May 28th.—Ditto.

May 29th.—Ditto.

May 30th.—Ditto.

May 31st.—Ditto.

June 1st.—E Company under Lieut. Boyall and 2nd Lieut. Clothier proceeded to Johannesburg Redoubt, and relieved H Company, who, under Lieut. Nicholson and 2nd Lieut. Shuttleworth, came into Head Quarters.

June 2nd.—No Church Parade on account of extreme cold. A very high and piercing wind all day. The detachment from Eerste Fabrieken, viz. :—D Company and practically all C Company, under Captain Trevor and 2nd Lieut. Wallace, rejoined Head Quarters.

June 3rd.—Nothing to record.

June 4th.—Ditto.

June 5th.—D Company, under Captain Trevor and 2nd Lieut. Otter, 2nd Norfolks (attached), relieved F Company, who, under Lieut. Lupton and 2nd Lieut. Keppell, of Norfolks (attached), returned to Head Quarters.

June 6th.—A Company, under Lieut. Cuthell, proceeded to Schantz Kopje Fort. Captain and Adjutant A. E. Daly left Head Quarters to take over command of a wing of the Victorian Mounted Rifles in Colonel Beatson's Column. Lieut. O. H. L. Nicholson took over the duties of Acting Adjutant.

June 7th.—A terrible railway accident, resulting in the death of nine Men and injuries to five others, all of the Regiment, took place at the

Camp at 5 a.m. this morning. An escort of 25 Men, under Lieut. Keppell, 2nd Norfolks (attached), was about to proceed to Nylstroom, and the train had drawn up in the cutting alongside the Camp in order to take them up. Owing to there not being room in the armoured truck for the whole escort, and natives having to be turned out of another truck to make room, there was a delay of some minutes. The Men were all just in the train, when the train following rushed round the curve behind and into the rear of the standing train. The armoured truck was completely telescoped, and several other carriages broken and derailed. A working party of the Regiment was quickly at work, and managed to get out the living quickly, with the exception of Private Shaw, who was under the wreck for two hours. The funeral of the Men was held in the afternoon in the cemetery.

Names of the Killed.

Lce.-Corporal Weston,	F Coy.		Private J. Jackson,	F Coy.
Private Rodwell,	F	,,	,, A. Ackroyd,	H ,,
,, R. Atkinson,	F	,,	,, M. Curley,	F ,,
,, J. Anderson,	F	,,	,, P. Redmond,	H ,,
,, D. Hope,	G	,,		

Injured, all more or less seriously.

Private A. Jones, 5894, F Coy.		Private J. Spellman, F Coy.	
,, T. Rowan,	H ,,	,, H. Shaw,	H ,,
,, H. Eshelby,	K ,,		

June 8th.—H Company, under 2nd Lieut. Shuttleworth, proceeded to take over Magazine Redoubt, Time Ball Hill, and blockhouse east of railway, from the Cameron Highlanders. D Company, under Captain Trevor, proceeded to Cable Hill, on being relieved at Daasrand West by F Company, under 2nd Lieut Lupton.

June 9th.—Sunday. No Church Parade, as there were very few Men left at Head Quarters, and these were on fatigue.

June 10th.—Nothing to record.

June 11th.—Ditto.

June 12th.—Captain Ingles returned from sick leave at Johannesburg. 2nd Lieut. Slade joined on first appointment, and was posted to C Company.

June 13th.—Nothing to record.

June 14th.—Ditto.

June 15th.—The Volunteer Service Company proceeded to the south-west Section, and took over all posts from Cantonments Site Blockhouse to Quaggapoort inclusive. E Company returned to Head Quarters; G Company, under Captain Ingles, relieved B Company at West Fort; B Company, under Lieut. P. E. H. Lowe, relieved F Company at Daasrand West; F Company returned to Head Quarters.

June 16th.—Sunday Service at St. Cuthbert's Church. Lieut. G. L. Crossman returned from sick leave.

June 17th.—A Company, under Lieut. Cuthell, returned to Head Quarters from Schantz Kop, being relieved by detachment of Gordons. 2nd Lieut. Shuttleworth returned to Head Quarters with Men of H Company from Magazine Redoubt and Time Ball Hill.

June 18th.—H Company, under 2nd Lieut. Shuttleworth, relieved B Company at Nos. 3 and 4 blockhouses, Daasrand Hill. 2nd Lieut. E. Grant-Dalton took the Men of B Company, thus relieved, to new post on kopje west of Sanitary Farm. During the night Captain Ingles took out a patrol from West Fort to intercept some Boers, who were looting sheep. A few shots were exchanged, No. 3058 Pte. E. Morris, B Company, being slightly wounded. The Boers got away, but left a large number of sheep behind them.

June 19th.—Nothing to record.

June 20th.—Orders to move to-morrow to new Camp near Proclamation Hill.

June 21st.—Marched to new Camp, west of Pretoria, between Mounted Infantry Depot and Proclamation Hill.

June 22nd.—B Company, from post near Sanitary Farm, returned to Head Quarters under Lieut. Lowe.

June 23rd.—Sunday Church Parade. Various posts of H Company and two posts of the Volunteers returned to Head Quarters, being relieved by the Gordons.

June 24th.—The Battalion (strength about 480) left the Camp standing and marched out, with 40 Canadian Scouts and 2 Guns Royal Horse Artillery, in a south-westerly direction. The Column was commanded by Lieut.-Colonel Fry. After a march of about seven miles, the Column halted for the night at Vlaakplaats, where it was joined by 100 Men, South African Constabulary. Got into signalling communication with Lieut.-Colonel Hackett-Thompson's Column, which was marching south from Rietfontein to Roodeval, and then in a north-easterly direction, to combine with our Column.

June 25th.—Marched at 2 a.m., and arrived in position near Hennop's River, closing the entrance of the valley of the Crocodile River. The valley runs far into the Schurveberg, and was used as the Head Quarters of the Pretoria Commando. Colonel Hackett-Thompson's Column, which was to have combined with us at day-break, was, at 8 o'clock, some six miles distant, and did not arrive till after 3 p.m., too late for any clearing operations in the valley.

Colonel Hackett-Thompson's Column had been strongly opposed by Boers on the 24th, hence the delay.

Major Ross (Canadian Scouts) and the South African Constabulary captured some cattle and sheep under fairly continuous sniping. About 130 Boers, with some large droves of cattle, were seen trekking in a westerly direction in the morning from between

3

the two Columns. The combined Columns, under Lieut.-Colonel W. Fry, bivouacked for the night on the position at the south end of the valley.

June 26th.—The Force paraded at 6-15 a.m. Major Watts, with some of the Imperial Yeomanry and B, E, and F Companies 2nd West Yorkshire Regiment, went back east with all baggage to some rising ground on the way to Vlaakplaats. The Cameron Highlanders, with 2 Guns Royal Field Artillery, took up a position commanding the approaches from the west, and overlooking the south-west of the valley. The rear of the Force was watched by the Volunteer Service Company West Yorkshire Regiment and Imperial Yeomanry. The Mounted Troops South African Constabulary, King's Royal Rifles, Mounted Infantry, and remainder of Canadian Scouts advanced into the valley, meeting with no opposition. The Canadian Scouts first moved out to the west to the Crocodile River, and then, clearing the country, swept round to the east, and moved up the valley. Having thoroughly cleared the valley, Major Ross advanced up the Kloofs of the Schurveberg in an easterly direction. Having finished the operation, the Force returned to Vlaakplaats with captured stock and wagons.

The rear guard was sniped for about an hour, but the Pom-pom kept the Boers at a distance. No casualties. The Force encamped at Vlaakplaats. As the Force retired the grass was set alight, so that all grazing was destroyed on the Schurveberg and along Hennaps River. The result of the operations was as follows :—

Burnt and thoroughly destroyed

250	Bags of wheat.	25	Wagons, with gear complete.
50	„ mealies.	6	Cape carts.
100	„ Kaffir corn.	4	Spiders.
2,500	Bundles oat hay.	30	Sets harness.
30	Bags flour.		

6 Dwelling-houses in which ammunition, &c., were found.
1 Grist mill, capable of turning out 3 bags a day.
Several saddles, bundles of clothing, &c., in laager.
1 Distillery.
Several farm implements.
About 500 rounds of ammunition and some coils of wire.
Captured and brought into Pretoria 690 head of cattle, 75 donkeys, about 1,500 sheep and goats, 4 mules.
And about 40 lung sick cattle destroyed, also some mules and horses not worth driving in.
2 Lee-Metford Rifles.
2 Mausers.

Families, &c.

12 Women, 32 children, and a Boer named Kock.

June 27th.—On orders received from Pretoria, Colonel Hackett-Thompson's Column marched back to Kalkheurel, beyond Rhenoster Kop, in the Schurveberg. The Canadian Scouts joined

3A

his Column, and the 112th Company Imperial Yeomanry joined Colonel Fry's Column. The latter returned to Pretoria with captured cattle, and arrived without opposition about 11-30 a.m. On arrival in Camp we found that an advanced party of about 50 Men, under Lieut. Welchman, had orders to proceed to Val (15 miles north of Standerton), by the 1-35 train. Orders received later that 2 Companies were to proceed on 28th, 2 Companies on 29th, and remainder on the 30th to Val.

June 28th.—F and H Companies, under Major Yale, proceeded by the 1-35 train for Val.

June 29th.—A and E Companies, under Lieut. Boyall, proceeded by the 1-35 train for Val.

June 30th.—Sunday. Head Quarters, with B, D, and G Companies left Pretoria by the 1-35 train. Stayed the night at Elandsfontein.

July 1st.—Head Quarters, with B, G, and D Companies, arrived at Val, and found A, E, F, and H Companies, under Major Yale, encamped. A and B Companies on outposts.

July 2nd.—Stayed at Val. Rejoined by C Company and Volunteer Service Company. Captain Carey stayed behind at Pretoria, having received orders to report himself to Army Pay Department, for duty. C and D Companies on outpost.

July 3rd.—Column consisted of West Yorkshire Regiment, 2 Guns T Battery Royal Horse Artillery, Mounted Infantry Company of Northamptons, 17 Field Company Royal Engineers. The whole, under the command of Lieut.-Colonel Fry, marched from Val station at 6 a.m. Major Yale took over command of Battalion from July 1st. The Force marched four miles. Building parties of the Royal Engineers and the West Yorkshires commenced building blockhouses near the Waterval stream, two miles, four miles, and six miles from Val. Garrisons, consisting of 12 N.C.O.'s and Men from A Company, were sent to each of these three posts, which were defensible by dusk, and connected by telegraph and telephone. The Force encamped at No. 2 blockhouse. During the day the Mounted Infantry patrols, about three miles in advance of No. 3 blockhouse, were engaged with a Force of the enemy. One Officer, four Men, and one Kaffir scout were wounded, and 20 in all were captured, but returned in the afternoon. Various bodies of the enemy were reported to the north-east and east, in some numbers. E, G, and K, Volunteer Service Company, on outposts, E Company holding a farm on the opposite side of the Val to the Camp.

July 4th.—About 3 a.m. E Company sent out an Officer's patrol, and fired at a party of six mounted Boers, who retreated shortly afterwards. Firing was heard from No. 3 blockhouse, from which it was reported that 30 Boers had retreated into the water-course. Parties completed the blockhouses.

In the afternoon orders were received to suspend operations for the present. F and H Companies on outpost. Notification received that Lieut.-Colonel Fry is posted to the command of the 2nd Battalion West Yorkshire Regiment, to date 23rd February, 1900.

The following was published in B. O. :—

"In making the above announcement, Lieut.-Colonel Fry begs to thank the Officers, N.C. Officers, and Men of the 2nd West Yorkshire Regiment, for their unvarying support. Lieut.-Colonel Fry largely attributes his good fortune, in obtaining the distinguished honour of commanding this gallant Corps, to the constant good conduct of all ranks, both on the march, in action, and in quarters."

July 5th.—Orders were received from Lord Kitchener. Nos. 2 and 3 blockhouses were pulled down. Orders for the Column to march back to Val and entrain for Potchefstroom. C and B Companies on outpost.

July 6th.—Force marched back to Val, after dismantling No. 1 blockhouse; arrived at Val about noon. Horses and mules of the Regiment were entrained at once, and were sent off with K Company at 4 p.m. One Section of T Battery Royal Horse Artillery followed with H Company as escort at 9 p.m. Fatigues were working during most of the night, entraining wagons, stores, &c. R, E, and D Companies on outpost.

July 7th.—Sunday. A Company started by train, leaving at 4 a.m. The Northamptonshire Mounted Infantry followed at 6 a.m. Colonel Fry, Major Watts and Staff, Major Yale, and B and E Companies left by the 8-30 a.m. train. The remainder of the Battalion under Captain Trevor left at 3 p.m. All trains travelling through the night, and only stopping about 10 minutes at Elandsfontein.

July 8th.—The last train of Troops arrived about 5 a.m. at Frederikstadt, where the whole Column re-assembled, with the exception of the Northamptonshire Mounted Infantry, who were detrained at Johannesburg, and A and K Companies and Section Royal Horse Artillery, who were sent on to Potchefstroom. Pitched Camp. F and G Companies on outpost.

July 9th.—Stayed at Camp at Frederikstadt. The Royal Horse Artillery and H and K Companies returned from Potchefstroom. Colonel Mackenzie's Column arrived. K Company on outpost.

July 10th.—Remained in Camp. The first blockhouse on the line along the Mooi River was built to-day near bridge to west of Frederikstadt. G and H Companies went to cover building, and were relieved by E and F Companies at noon. Garrison of 12 N.C.O.'s and Men, A Company, took up the post. H Company on outpost.

July 11th.—Struck Camp and marched with the Column from Frederikstadt at 8 a.m. D, E, and F Companies advanced and flank guards under Captain Trevor. Commenced No. 2 blockhouse about two miles above No. 1 on the Mooi River. Bivouacked near it. B and C Companies on outpost.

July 12th.—Marched at 6-15 a.m., and halted for bivouac about three and a-half miles from No. 2 blockhouse. Finished No. 2 and commenced Nos. 3 and 4. B, G, and K Companies advance guard. Lieut. Shuttleworth left the Battalion on his way to England, *en route* for India, on transfer to Indian Staff Corps. No. 4 blockhouse and the present Camp overlook the village of Muiskraal. D and E Companies on outposts. A few Boers left the end of the village as A and G Companies entered.

July 13th.—The Force remained in Camp. Nos. 2 and 4 blockhouses completed. The Boers set alight all the grazing ground to the north of us in the plain. We burnt a strip in front of the Camp to prevent the fire reaching us. F and E Companies on outposts.

July 14th.—Sunday. G, H, and K Companies remained in Camp, though the remains of the Force marched out at 6-15 a.m. and commenced Nos. 5 and 6 blockhouses—No. 5 at north-east end of village, No. 6 about two miles further on, near bridge over the Mooi River. No opposition. About 12 Boers seen near Reitvlei Nek. The blockhouses were completed at dusk, and the Force returned to Camp at No. 4. A and K Companies on outpost.

July 15th.—The Force marched out at 6-15 a.m. Lieut. Lemon was left at No. 4 blockhouse, Nos. 1, 2, 3, 4, and 5 being garrisoned by A Company. Lieut. Hirst, Volunteer Company, was left at No. 6 with Garrison of Volunteer Company. The Force marched to Rooidraai Farm, and encamped there, building No. 7 blockhouse about one and a-half miles from No. 6; Nos. 8 and 9 were commenced at Rooidraai, K Company supplying Garrison of Nos. 7, 8, and 9. Fortifications were also commenced at the Camp, as a Garrison of about 100 Men, consisting of G Company and the two Garrisons of K Company under Captain Ingles and Captain Pearson (Volunteer Service Company) are to stay here. A few Boers further along the Mooi River in the next village. Colonel Mackenzie's Column arrived from Frederikstadt, and camped with us. B Company on outpost.

July 16th.—C and G Companies under Captain Ingles marched at 7 a.m. with empty wagons for Frederikstadt. Colonel Mackenzie's Column continued their march at 10-30 a.m. B and H Companies went out as covering and working parties for No. 10 blockhouse Remainder of Force stayed in Camp. Nos. 8 and 9 blockhouses completed. No. 10 commenced about two miles further on. Colonel Mackenzie's Column are building Nos. 12, 13, and 14 for us. Men were left in Camp, and were on fatigue all day, fortifying the post. D Company on outpost.

July 17th.—Force remained in Camp. ½ B and F Companies went out as covering and working parties for the building of No. 11 blockhouse. They returned at dusk. Captain Ingles returned with full Convoy from Frederikstadt.

July 18th.—Lieut. Crossman with H Company escorted empty wagons to Frederikstadt. The Column marched out at 6-5 a.m., leaving

G Company under Captain Ingles as Garrison of the post. We passed Colonel Mackenzie's Column at No. 13 blockhouse. Commenced Nos. 15 and 16, and encamped at the latter at Varkens Kraal. Colonel Mackenzie arrived at the same Camp in the afternoon. F Company on outpost.

July 19th.—The Force remained in Camp. Nos. 15 and 16 blockhouses completed. No. 17 commenced. G and F Companies went out as working and covering parties. C Company on outpost. Colonel Mackenzie continued his march.

July 20th.—The Force remained in Camp. No. 17 blockhouse completed, No. 18 commenced; E and C Companies went out as covering and working parties. Lieut. Crossman returned with full Convoy, and went out to the Eye of Mooi River, where Colonel Mackenzie's Column is. "A" post is to be established there, H Company furnishing the Garrison. 24 N.C.O.'s and Men of C Company went out with H Company as Garrison for the two blockhouses of the post. G Company on outpost.

July 21st.—Sunday. Force started at 8 a.m. with Convoy of empty wagons for Frederikstadt, C and D Companies advanced and flank guards. Arrived at "A" post about 1 o'clock. One Company of 11th Mounted Infantry joined the Force there. E Company on outpost.

July 22nd.—Started from "A" post at 7 a.m., and a little after 1 p.m. we arrived at Frederikstadt. E and F Companies advanced, rear, and flank guards. F Company on outpost.

July 23rd.—Halted at Frederikstadt and loaded up wagons. C Company on outpost.

July 24th.—Started from Frederikstadt with full Convoy. Arrived at "A" post about 1 p.m. C and D Companies formed advanced, flank, and rear guards.

July 25th.—Marched at 7 a.m., and arrived at post "B," near the Eye of the Mooi, about 2 p.m. A march of about 14 miles. Colonel Mackenzie's Column still here. E and F Companies formed the advanced, rear, and flank guards. D Company on outpost.

July 26th.—Halted at "B" post: the Suffolks moved on. C Company took up Nos. 21, 22, and 23 blockhouses, No. 23 being the last one to be held by the Regiment. E Company on outpost.

July 27th.—Halted at "B" post., work in the morning, improving the wire fences and trying to destroy the thick cover on the river bank. E Company went out in the afternoon to meet the empty Convoy returning from Colonel Mackenzie's Column. F Company on outpost.

July 28th.—Force marched at 7 a.m. G and F Companies formed advanced, flank, and rear guards. Encamped for the night at "A" post.

July 29th.—Force marched at 7 a.m., G and F Companies advanced, flank, and rear guards. D Company on outpost. Arrived at Frederikstadt with the empty Convoy about 3 p.m.

July 30th.—Force remained at Frederikstadt. E Company on outpost.

July 31st.—Force marched at 7 a.m. with full Convoy, E and F Companies advanced, flank, and rear guards. Encamped for the night at "A" post. Kaffirs there report that Wolmarans is going to arrive at Reitvlei Nek to-night.

August 1st.—Force marched at 7 a.m., F and B Companies advanced, flank, and rear guards. Arrived at "B" post about 2 p.m. F Company on outpost.

August 2nd.—Force halted at "B" post. F and D Companies marched with Convoy for Colonel Mackenzie's Column. Handed it over near No. 24 blockhouse. Captain Ingles reported no further news of Wolmarans. D Company on outpost.

August 3rd.—Force remained at "B" post, but E and F Companies, the Section of Royal Horse Artillery, and the Mounted Infantry Section went to meet the empty Convoy returning from Colonel Mackenzie's Column, which is now about nine miles from Naaupoort. They met the Convoy near No. 24 blockhouse, and returned to "B" post. Kemp's Commando reported about 20 miles from here. E Company on outpost.

August 4th.—Force marched at 7 a.m. with empty Convoy, D and E Companies advanced, flank, and rear guards. Arrived at "A" post about 1 p.m.

August 5th.—Marched at 7 a.m., E and F Companies advanced, flank, and rear guards. Arrived at Frederikstadt about 1-30 p.m. F Company on outpost.

August 6th.—Halted at Frederikstadt. D Company on outpost.

August 7th.—Halted at Frederikstadt. E Company on outpost.

August 8th.—Force marched at 7 a.m., F and D Companies advanced, flank, and rear guards. Arrived at "A" post about 1-30 p.m.

August 9th.—Force marched from "A" post at 7 a.m. During an outspan between Nos. 16 and 17 blockhouses it was reported that about 60 Boers were riding over the hills on east of river towards No. 13 blockhouse; we could see them from the column, about 5,000 yards away. They suddenly turned round and galloped away towards the east, as if fired upon. Sergt. Warwick, No. 13 blockhouse, afterwards reported that he had fired on them at 1,000 yards, and that they scattered and fled away, leaving two riderless horses. Kaffirs say that one Boer was wounded. Arrived at "B" post about 3 p.m. F Company on outpost.

August 10th.—Captain Ingles reported this morning by wire that he captured two Boers last night. 2 Companies of the Suffolks which had come into "B" post left with the Convoy. Force halted. D Company on outpost.

August 11th.—Force halted. D and E Companies marched to meet empty Convoy at No. 24 blockhouse. E Company on outpost.

August 12th.—Force marched with empty Convoy at 6-45 a.m. There was a certain amount of firing heard from different posts about 5-30 a.m. No. 22 blockhouse fired at three Boers, and patrol, returning to "B" post from night duty, fired a couple of volleys at Boers they said they saw to the west. Sergt. Warwick at No. 13 reported that the two horses they wounded on the 9th were afterwards shot as useless. Force halted for the night at "A" post.

August 13th.—Force marched at 6-45 a.m., and arrived at Frederikstadt about 1 p.m. Brought in the two Boers captured by 10 men under Cr.-Sergt. Kingsley, sent out by Captain Ingles. F Company on outpost.

August 14th.—Force halted at Frederikstadt. D Company on outpost. Captain Ingles reported the surrender of one burgher of Kemp's Commando, and the finding of two Rifles and Ammunition.

August 15th.—Force halted. E Company on outpost.

August 16th.—Force marched with full Convoy at 6-45 a.m. Halted for the night at "A" post. D and E Companies advanced, flank, and rear guards.

August 17th.—Force marched at 6-45 a.m., and halted for the night at "B" post. E and F Companies advanced, flank, and rear guards. F Company on outpost.

August 18th.—Force marched at 6-45 a.m., and halted at "C" post (Elandsfontein) held by the Suffolks. A march of $14\frac{1}{4}$ miles. F and D Companies advanced, flank, and rear guards.

August 19th.—F and D Companies, with Mounted Infantry, marched with the Convoy, which was handed over to the Suffolks near No. 35 blockhouse, about four miles short of Naaupoort. The 2 Companies then returned to "C" post. E Company on outpost.

August 20th.—Force marched at 6-45 a.m., and halted for the night at "B" post. D and E Companies advanced, flank, and rear guards. D Company on outpost.

August 21st.—Force marched with empty Convoy at 6-15 a.m. Halted for two hours near No. 16 blockhouse, while bad bit of road was being repaired. Arrived at "A" post about 1 p.m. E and F Companies advanced, flank, and rear guards.

August 22nd.—Force marched at 6-15 a.m., and arrived at Frederikstadt about 12 noon. F and D Companies advanced, flank, and rear guards. 2nd Lieut. D. Grant-Dalton joined on first appointment, and posted to G Company. F Company on outpost.

August 23rd.—Force halted at Frederikstadt. D Company on outpost.

August 24th.—Force halted at Frederikstadt. 2nd Lieut. H. E. G. Bird, from the Cape Mounted Rifles, joined on first appointment, and was posted to H Company. E Company on outpost. Good rain in the afternoon.

August 25th.—Force started with full Convoy from Frederikstadt, D and E Companies advanced, flank, and rear guards. Halted for the night at " A " post.

August 26th.—Force continued the march at 6-15 a.m., and arrived at " B " post about 1 p.m. E and F Companies advanced, flank, and rear guards. H Company on outpost. Major-General Willson, commanding Krugersdorp district, arrived from Naaupoort on a tour of inspection, and stayed for the night.

August 27th.—The Force halted at " B " post. Major Yale, with E Company, took on some mule wagons, with supplies for A Section of the Suffolks, to "C" post. F Company took over Nos. 25, 26, 27, and 28 blockhouses from the Suffolk Regiment. D Company at work repairing the road.

August 28th.—Major Yale returned with empty wagons for " C " post. Force halted at " B " post.

August 29th.—Force halted at " B " post. D Company on outpost.

August 30th.—Force started on the march for Frederikstadt at 6-15 a.m., D Company advanced, flank, and rear guards. Halted for the night at " A " post.

August 31st.—Marched at 6-15 a.m., and arrived at Frederikstadt. E Company advanced, flank, and rear guards. E Company on outpost.

September 1st.—Sunday. Halted at Frederikstadt. D Company on outpost. The Section of T Battery Royal Horse Artillery, under Lieut. Synnott, left the Column to join Colonel Romilly's Column at Potchefstroom.

September 2nd.—Remained at Frederikstadt. E Company on outpost.

September 3rd.—Force marched from Frederikstadt at 6-15 a.m. with full Convoy, D Company advanced, flank, and rear guards. Arrived at " A " post about noon.

September 4th.—Force halted at " A " post. Lieut. Boyall, with E Company, took over the post from Captain Ingles, with G Company.

September 5th.—Force continued the march. Arrived at " B " post about 1 p.m. G Company advanced, flank, and rear guards.

September 6th.—Force halted at " B " post. Captain Trevor, with D Company, took over the post from Lieut. Crossman, with H Company.

September 7th.—H Company, with the Mounted Infantry, marched for " C " post with Convoy. A burgher, Van Lingen, surrendered to 2nd Lieut. Welchman at No. 16 blockhouse, and was sent on to " C " post. He was carrying a despatch from Commandant Lichtenberg to Commandant De la Rey, and gave much interesting information.

September 8th.—Halted at " B " post. Convoy returned from " C " post.

September 9th.—Halted at "B" post.

September 10th.—Ditto.

September 11th.—Marched with empty Convoy from "B" post for Frederikstadt, H Company advanced, flank, and rear guards. Halted for the night at "A" post.

September 12th.—Marched at 6-15 a.m., and arrived at Frederikstadt about noon. Orders to take over the fortifications from the Coldstream Guards. H Company took over the two blockhouses on Gun Hill and the bridge guard. Major Yale appointed Commandant, and Lieut. Crossman R.S.O. and Camp Adjutant.

September 13th.—G Company took over three blockhouses on South Hill from the Border Regiment (Volunteer Service Company). Worked all day improving defences.

September 14th.—At work improving defences. 2nd Lieut. Harrington returned from Convalescent Camp, Howick.

September 15th.—Sunday. Lieut. Francis left with Convoy for blockhouse line; escort of 20 Men of G Company as far as No. 4 blockhouse, where the duty of escort was taken over by Lieut. Boyall with 25 Men of E Company from "A" post. At work on the defences. 2nd Lieut. Harrington went out to assume command of C Company. "The Guards" were to have left to-day, but no train accommodation was available. To-day is the last day on which the Boers can surrender under Lord Kitchener's proclamation.

September 16th.—"The Guards" left this morning. The formation of the Camp is altered, the whole thing being rendered more compact in a ring fence, and fresh works commenced.

September 17th.—At work on the defences in the morning and afternoon.

September 18th.—Bandmaster Finigan, with the band, drums, instruments, and Boys, arrived from Krugersdorp. At work on the defences.

September 19th.—At work on the defences.

September 20th.—Ditto.

September 21st.—At work on the defences in the morning.

September 22nd.—Sunday. Church Parade in the morning.

September 23rd.—At work on the defences in the morning. Colonel Hicks' Column came into Frederikstadt in the afternoon, bringing eight prisoners and many Boer families.

September 24th.—Colonel Hicks' Column left this morning. The Battalion received orders by wire to concentrate here at Frederikstadt as soon as possible. The King's Own Scottish Borderers to relieve us.

September 25th.—Orders received for the Battalion to be railed to Volksrust, Company by Company as relieved. Three Men per blockhouses Nos. 1 to 12 and 20 of E Company marched in.

September 26th.—Head Quarters of Battalion (about 146 Men), most of the transport, left by special train at 2-30 p.m.; reached Elandsfontein at 10-15 p.m., and stayed in the train there.

September 27th.—Volksrust. Left Elandsfontein at 4 a.m., and arrived at Volksrust at 9-15 p.m. Remained at station for the night.

September 28th.—Unloaded the train at 6 a.m., and marched about one mile to the west of the town, where the Camp was pitched. The West Yorkshires and Scots Guards are to build a line of block-houses from Wakkerstroom through Piet Retief to the Swaziland border. 2nd Lieut. Clothier and 66 Men arrived by train this evening.

September 29th.—Volksrust. Sunday. 4 Officers and more Men arrived about noon. 16 Officers and the remainder of the Men, numbering about 550, arrived in the evening. The band and time-expired Men were sent to the Details Camp. Orders to march to-morrow at 5-45 a.m.

September 30th.—The Column marched at 5-45 a.m., the Scots Guards furnishing advanced guard, then 3 Companies of the Queen's, Royal Engineers, and the 2nd West Yorkshires furnishing the rear guard and flank guards for mule Convoy, then the Mounted Troops, viz., 1 Squadron 8th Hussars, 1 Section Queen's Mounted Infantry, 1 Section Scots Guards Mounted Infantry. Arrived at Wakkerstroom about 4 p.m., after an uneventful march. A and B Companies on outpost.

October 1st.—Goudhoek. Marched at 6 a.m. C and D Companies advanced guard from Wakkerstroom. Six blockhouses were commenced and were defensible by nightfall. The Volunteer Service Company under Captain W. A. Pearson furnished the Garrisons. No. 1 blockhouse was built on high hill, north-west of Noude Farm, and the others north and south of the main road from Wakkerstroom to Piet Retief, which is the line to be guarded. The working parties were furnished by the Battalion. The Battalion encamped on high ground overlooking Goudhoek. The Scots Guards encamped about two miles further on towards Castrol Nek, while the Queen's held the Nek. B and D Companies on outpost.

October 2nd.—All Companies were on working fatigue. By noon blockhouses Nos. 1 to 6 were completed, and No. 7 was completed and Nos. 8 and 9 in a state of defence by dusk. The Battalion went on to Castrol Nek, and encamped there for the night. General Bullock and the remainder of the Force went on about three miles. A thick fog came on at dusk. D and E Companies on outpost.

October 3rd.—The fog continued till noon, which rather hampered the work. C Company went on and commenced Nos. 12 and 13 blockhouses. Nos. 10 and 11 were commenced on Tafel Kop. A Company went back and completed Nos. 8 and 9. The work of putting the Nek and Tafel Kop into a state of defence was commenced at 1-30 p.m. The Battalion marched, leaving F, G, and H Companies, under the command of Captain Ingles, as Garrison of Castrol Nek and Tafel Kop. No. 14 blockhouse was commenced in the afternoon. The Battalion marched about four miles and encamped at Naaugevonden. A Company on outpost. Nos. 12, 13, and 14 blockhouses were garrisoned by B Company.

October 4th.—Nos. 12, 13, and 14 blockhouses were finished early : Nos. 15, 16, 17, 18, 19, and 20 were commenced, and by dusk were all nearly completed, or at least in a state of defence. Nos. 15, 16, and 17 blockhouses were garrisoned by B Company, Lieut. Welchman being posted at No. 15, which commands the valley running from Paul Pietersberg to Castrol Nek. Nos. 18, 19, and 20 blockhouses were garrisoned by C Company. The remainder of the Battalion marched at 1-30 p.m., and encamped for the night near the Mabola River, near Johnson's Farm. No. 21 blockhouse was completed. D and C Companies on outpost.

October 5th.—Nos. 21, 22A, sangar on Necklace Kop, 23 and 24 were commenced and completed, or in state of defence by dusk. All these posts with the exception of No. 24 were garrisoned by C Company. Lieut. Harrington was posted at Necklace Kop, a sugarloaf-shaped hill commanding the country to the north. The remainder of the Battalion marched at 1-30 p.m., and encamped about four miles further on at Vergelegan, where the second post is. A Garrison of 24 of A Company was sent out to a hill one and a-half miles to the north-west, fortified with blockhouses (No. 25 and two sangars), No. 24 garrisoned by E Company. E Company on outpost.

October 6th.—A Company sent out Garrison to blockhouses Nos. 26 and 27 and two sangars (one numbered 28). D and E Companies remain as Garrison of this post. Work in the morning fortifying the post. Convoy for Volksrust left.

October 7th.—Head Quarters of the Regiment marched for Castrol Nek, leaving Major Yale in command of No. 2 post. It is reported that Louis Botha is heading north again from the direction of Natal. A thick fog came on at dusk.

October 8th.—Castrol Nek. A thick fog necessitated the outpost being out all day. Convoys arrived from both directions.

October 9th.—Heavy rain all day. Major E. Layton, on promotion from South Stafford Regiment, joined the Battalion, and was posted to the command of C Company. A Guide, Mr. De Jager, with native scouts, arrived for duty at this post. Rain and mist all day.

October 10th.—Major Layton left for " B " post this morning. Convoys in and out. Heavy rain and mist. The report of the great defeat of the Boers at Itala and the Mount Prospect is confirmed. The Boer losses seem to be at least 200 killed.

October 11th.—A large Convoy, coming in here from Wakkerstroom, was delayed by the weather, and halted for the night at No. 9 blockhouse. Very heavy rain.

October 12th.—The Convoy came in to-day. Very wet.

October 13th.—General Plumer's Column arrived here to-day, to take part in the operation in this neighbourhood. The main body of the Boers seemed to be near Luneburg and the Pongola Bosch. A party of 12 Men of G Company was sent out this afternoon to build and occupy a sangar between Nos. 18 and 20 blockhouses, on the Helpmakaar Road, where it is possible the Boers may break through. 150 Mounted Men from General Plumer's Column went out later to support them.

October 14th.—Empty Convoy left for Wakkerstroom. General Plumer's Column marched out, but only went as far as No. 15 blockhouse, in consequence of information which tended to show that the Boers were trying to break west. No. 7 blockhouse had some firing at Boers trying to round up some horses to the north, and kept them off. At night five Men were sent to Nos. 8 and 9 blockhouses, each for reinforcement, as it was possible that a large body might attempt the passage between those blockhouses and Nos. 6 and 7. No attempt was made. The signallers got into communication with General W. Kitchener, who had moved to Tugela, at Paul Pietersberg.

October 15th.—General Plumer's Column's Camp stayed at same place, but his Force went out and got into touch with the enemy. The signallers again in communication with General W. Kitchener.

October 16th.—G Company took over Nos. 12, 13, and 14 blockhouses from B Company. B Company took over Nos. 18 and 19 from C Company. C Company took over new sangar No. 20.

The following order was published in Battalion Orders: "The King has been graciously pleased to give orders for the following appointments to the Most Honourable Order of the Bath, and the Distinguished Service Order for the following promotions in the Army, and for the grant of the Medal for distinguished conduct in the field, to the undermentioned Officers and Soldiers. in recognition of their services during the operations in South Africa. The whole to bear dates 29th November, 1900, except where otherwise stated:—

2ND BATTALION P.W.O. WEST YORKSHIRE REGIMENT.

To be a Companion of the Order of the Bath :—
    Lieut.-Colonel William Fry.

To be a Companion of the Distinguished Service Order :—
    Major James Corbett Yale.
    Lieut. Sydney Goodall Francis.
    Lieut. Octavius Henry Lothian Nicholson.
    Lieut. Alfred Morley Boyall.

To be Brevet Lieut.-Colonel :—
 Major H. E. Watts.
To be Brevet Major :—
 Captain W. S. Carey.
To have the Distinguished Conduct Medal :—
 No. 1812 Cr.-Sergt. E. Busher,   E Company.
 „ 3325 Sergt. J. Walmsley,   F   „
 „ 2291 Lce.-Corpl. J. Rownsley, D   „
 „ 5373 Lce.-Corpl. F. Scott,   G   „
 „ 2924 Private A Powell,   E   „
 „ 5090 Private J. Banks,   A   „
 „ 5171 Private B. Woodhead,   B   „

SOUTH STAFFORD REGIMENT.
To be a Companion of the Distinguished Service Order :—
 Captain E. Layton, now Major 2nd West Yorks. Regt."

October 17th.—The signallers were in communication again with General Walter Kitchener, who appears to be now marching towards Luneburg. The Column all seem to be closing up round the Slangapies and Pongola Bosch. General Pulteney's Column was seen to the south-east, and was afterwards reported fighting in the Pongola Bosch. Convoys in and out. Captain Trevor and 40 Men, D Company, marched from "B" post to "C" post at St. Helena, which place, according to native, was to be attacked this night.

October 18th.—A thick fog, which kept the outpost out all day, and also prevented any signalling with General Kitchener. Empty Convoy went into Wakkerstroom, and full one returned.

October 19th.—The fog continued all day. In the evening General Plumer wired that he was sending up 300 cattle from Geluk to his Camp near No. 15 blockhouse.

October 20th.—Rain and fog again to-day. The captured cattle and about half a dozen prisoners passed through to-day.

October 21st.—A fairly fine day, but it was never possible to get into signalling communication with Columns, as there was very little sun. Various Convoys in both directions.

October 22nd.—A very thick fog all day. Major Cayley with a draft from England of 72 N.C.O.'s and Men arrived in the evening. They had been employed on Column over three weeks under Colonel Mills, at Greystown, Natal. It is reported that many Boers have broken north. 2nd Lieut. Welchman made an expedition from No. 15 blockhouse to capture three Boers, of whom natives had given information. He found that with his small Force he was getting away too far, so his small Force returned about 1 a.m.

October 23rd.—The Commanding Officer inspected the draft in the morning. The Men were afterwards apportioned out to their Companies in such a way as to make each Company present about 80 strong.

October 24th.—2nd Lieut. Welchman with 12 Men made a night march of about four or five miles, and captured two armed Boers and 13 women and children in a kloof. At daybreak, on his way back, he also captured an unarmed Boer. He got them back to his blockhouse about noon, and they arrived at Castrol Nek at dusk. He also captured about 200 rounds of small-arm ammunition with two Lee-Metford rifles. The draft, with the exception of G and H Companies, marched at 6-30 a.m. with Major Cayley, *en route* for their various Companies. Major Cayley assumed command of F Company at "C" post.

October 25th.—Seven Boer prisoners arrived from General Plumer, who had gone down again into the Pongola Bosch. General Plumer sent a congratulatory telegram to the Commanding Officer on Lieut. Welchman's capture. He says, "I consider it reflects the greatest credit on 2nd Lieut. Welchman and the Men with him." Major Kent arrived in the afternoon with a Naval 12-pounder Gun for duty here. It was placed on the top of Tafel Kop.

October 26th.—2nd Lieut. Welchman, with 12 Men, again effected a capture of three armed Boers, with ammunition, five horses, and one mule, by lying in ambush at night at a drift by which, from information by Kaffirs, he knew the Boers were going to attempt to pass.

October 27th.—The three prisoners were brought in here from No. 15 blockhouse. Very foggy and wet weather.

October 28th.—Eighteen prisoners were sent in from General Plumer; they included Field Cornet Breytenbach. A fresh Garrison of 10 Men was sent out to take over No. 32 blockhouse from the Scots Guards.

October 29th.—The prisoners were sent into Wakkerstroom under escort. General Lyttelton sent the Commanding Officer congratulatory message on Lieut. Welchman.

October 30th.—A perfect hurricane blew all day, the greater part of the tents had to be struck as they were all being torn. Colonel Fry took 150 Q.I.B. and Hants. M.I. (of General Plumer), and 30 of the 8th Hussars, to locate the Boers to the north, in the direction of Derdehoek, and, if possible, to drive them on to the Columns to the north-west. The Boers were found to be in some strength, and there were no signs of any columns to the north. The Force returned about 4 p.m. No casualties.

October 31st.—General Plumer's detached Force of Q.I.B. and Hants. M.I. went forward to join him at Zuikerhoek. Ten more men of the Battalion went forward to garrison No. 33 blockhouse.

November 1st.—Two Men on escort from "B" post (Mabola) were wounded by No. 28 blockhouse, both severely, one in the arm and the other in the ankle. Court of Enquiry held at Mabola.

November 2nd.—General Bullock arrived at Castrol Nek, the block-houses being completed. A large Convoy coming in from Wakkerstroom was delayed by the weather, and a considerable portion of it had to remain on the road near No. 9 blockhouse.

November 3rd.—Sunday. General Bullock left this morning for Volks-rust. Service in the morning.

November 4th.—Ten Men left Castrol for " B " post, to take up a new blockhouse to be built between Nos. 28 and 29 blockhouses.

November 5th.—The following order of General Bullock was published in Battalion Orders:—

" The following telegram has been received from Commander-in-Chief. Brigadier-General Bullock does not view it as a personal compliment, so much as a tribute of the high quality of the Troops he has had the honour of commanding during the recent erection of blockhouses.

' 4th November. K 8390.

" I am much pleased with energy and good work of General Bullock and Troops employed under him on blockhouse construc-tion. All deserve great credit for results obtained under such difficult conditions, and I hope line will now be made an effective barrier.' "

The following was published in Orders on 27th October :—

" The King has been graciously pleased to signify his intention to confer the decoration of the Victoria Cross on the undernamed N.C.O., whose claims have been submitted for His Majesty's approval, for his conspicuous bravery in South Africa as stated against his name.

2ND BATTALION WEST YORKSHIRE REGIMENT.

Sergeant W. B. Traynor.

During the night attack on Bothwell Camp on 6th February, 1901, jumped out of a trench, and ran out under an extremely heavy fire to the assistance of a wounded man. While running out he was severely wounded, and, being unable to carry the man by himself, he called for assistance. Lance-Corporal Lintott at once came to him, and between them they carried the wounded soldier into shelter. After this, although severely wounded, Sergeant Traynor remained in command of his Section, and was most cheerful in encouraging his Men until the attack failed."

" His Majesty has been further pleased to approve of the grant of the Medal for Distinguished Conduct in the Field to the undermentioned soldier, in recognition of his gallant conduct during the recent operations in South Africa :—

No. 2983 Corporal W. T. Lintott, 2nd West Yorks. Regiment, *vide London Gazette*, Tuesday, September 17th, 1901."

November 6th.—2nd Lieuts. Smart and Fisher arrived on first appointment, and were posted to A and F Companies respectively.

November 7th.—Nothing of interest.

November 8th.—A very heavy thunderstorm with hail in the afternoon and evening. Four horses and several mules of General Plumer's Column at Mabola were killed. Nos. 19, 16, and 15 blockhouses were all fired at in the night, and it is believed that about 30 Boers passed from north to south between Nos. 13 and 14 blockhouses.

November 9th.—Another very heavy thunderstorm in the early part of the night. Private Smith, H Company, was struck by lightning while on sentry duty on Gun Hill; he was blinded, and lost the use of his legs, but the doctor thinks that both injuries are only temporary.

It was reported that Botha and a few Men passed from south to north between Nos. 22 and 23 blockhouses.

November 10th.—Sunday. Another heavy storm at night, during which one horse and four mules were killed.

November 11th.—Boers tried to cross from south to north between Nos. 22 and 23 blockhouses, but were seen by the former, who were warned by black scout, and were driven back. Private Evans missing from No. 21 blockhouse since 9 a.m.

November 12th.—Captain Ingles left the Battalion this morning *en route* for York, where he takes over the Adjutancy of the 1st Volunteer Battalion West Yorkshire Regiment. 2nd Lieut. D. Grant-Dalton took over command of G Company. Private Evans was found this afternoon by a patrol of General Plumer's Column and was brought back. A new sangar built between Nos. 22 and 23 blockhouses. News received of capture of a few Boers, several horses, small-arm ammunition, and rifles, near "C" post, Amsterdam.

November 13th.—General Plumer's Column, which had been encamped for two days under No. 20 blockhouse, went forward to Amsterdam.

November 14th.—A new sangar, garrisoned by G Company, commenced between Nos. 13 and 14 blockhouses. Wire fence between blockhouses also commenced.

November 15th.—Eight prisoners were sent in from "C" post, near which they had been captured by part of Plumer's Force, guided by scouts from the post.

November 16th.—A new sangar, garrisoned by G Company, was commenced between Nos. 14 and 15 blockhouses.

November 17th.—The Men had a day's rest from fatigues. The Sappers and Natives commenced a new blockhouse to the west of Nos. 8 and 9; it was defensible by nightfall, and garrisoned by the Volunteers.

November 18th.—2nd Lieut. Welchman, with 12 Men of B Company and 10 from Castrol Nek, made a night raid. A party of 7 Boers, with some women and children, had been marked down in a kloof by his native scouts. About 8 p.m. he started, but found that the Boers had moved into the Pongola Bosch, about seven miles further on. He was guided into the bush by his scouts, and by daybreak he had their hiding surrounded. None of the party escaped, and his total captures were:—8 Boers, 3 women, 9 children, 120 rounds small-arm ammunition, 10 horses, saddles, &c., about 50 head of cattle, 150 sheep and goats ; 2 wagons were burnt. 25 Men of the 8th Hussars went down into the valley below No. 15 blockhouse at daybreak in case they should be required, but they were not called upon.

The party arrived back at No. 15 blockhouse about mid-day the 19th, having covered about 26 miles since 8 p.m. on the 18th.

November 19th.—The prisoners taken by Lieut. Welchman in the early part of this morning were brought into Castrol. General Bullock wired to say he was very pleased with Lieut. Welchman, and sent his congratulations.

November 20th.—A detachment of General Plumer's Force arrived in the afternoon, and went out again at night, to try and capture Stoffel Botha and other Boers, near Farm Geluk, about six miles north-west of Frere.

November 21st.—General Plumer's Colonials were successful in capturing Stoffel Botha and six other Boers early this morning. 2nd Lieut. Welchman received the following telegram from General Lord Kitchener of Khartoum:—

"21st November. K 8724.
"I am very glad to hear such satisfactory report of your expeditions. Tell the Men that went with you I am much pleased with their success."

November 22nd.—A very heavy wind all day. Nothing to record.

November 23rd.—Trench between Castrol Nek and No. 12 sangar commenced.

November 24th.—Sunday. There were no fatigues to-day. Major Cayley wired from "C" post that six Boers had surrendered to him.

November 25th.—Wire fence between No. 12 sangar and Castrol Nek commenced.

November 26th.—2nd Lieut. Welchman started at 8 p.m. with 25 Men to raid four Boers in the Pongola Bosch, about 14 miles from his blockhouse.

November 27th.—2nd Lieut. Welchman rushed the Boers just before dawn. On account of the fineness of the night, the Boers were sleeping outside, and a dog barking gave two of them the warning. Two Boers and three rifles were captured, and a few women and children brought in. The prisoners were brought to Head Quarters in the evening.

November 28th.—Another Boer surrendered to Major Cayley at "C" post. The usual work at fences.

November 29th.—The usual fatigues. The fine weather we were having this week broke up in the afternoon.

November 30th.—Secret despatches were sent out by relays of Mounted Officers to General Plumer and Colonels Pulteney and Colville.

December 1st.—Sunday. The wire fence from Castrol Nek to "B" post complete. The curtain on the north side of it also complete.

December 2nd.—Brigadier-General Bullock with 30 of 8th Hussars and 2 Guns, 53rd Battery Royal Field Artillery, arrived from Volksrust and remained here for the night.

December 3rd.—Brigadier-General Bullock left in the morning for "B" post. Very heavy rain all day.

December 4th.—The usual fatigues.

December 5th.—Ditto.

December 6th.—Ditto.
We were in communication, from Paarde Kop, with Plumer's and Pulteney's Columns in the direction of Beelzebub.

December 7th.—28 Men of the North Staffordshire Mounted Infantry and 20 Men under Lieut. Crossman went out to Johnson's Hoek to cover the Convoy from Wakkerstroom to General Plumer and Colonel Pulteney. A great many Boers were seen in the Waaihoek Valley.

December 8th.—Sunday. Brigadier-General Bullock arrived in the afternoon from "C" post. A new blockhouse to west of No. 1 was built, and garrisoned by Men of the Volunteer Company. There are now three blockhouses between Wakkerstroom and No. 1 blockhouse, the two nearer Wakkerstroom being garrisoned by the North Staffords.

December 9th.—Brigadier-General Bullock left in the morning for Volksrust. Boers are reported to the number of 300 in the Waaihoek. In the evening 2nd Lieut. Welchman reported the arrival of some numbers at Mooi Plaats, seven miles north of his blockhouse. Usual fatigues.

December 10th.—2nd Lieut. Welchman reported that 100 Boers arrived at Mooi Plaats last evening, and then went west during the night, in direction of Wakkerstroom Hills, but returned east again. The usual fatigues.

December 11th.—The Boers are reported to have left the Waaihoek Valley. The signallers on Paarde Kop could not get communication with any Columns to the north. The usual fatigues and H Company rifle practice from the loopholes of the blockhouses and sangars on Gun Hill.

December 12th.—The usual fatigue. News received of large captures by General Bruce Hamilton and Colonel Colenbrander.

December 13th.—The usual fatigues and rifle practice from sangars in the Nek.

December 14th.—The usual fatigues.

December 15th.—No fatigues. Sunday Service in the morning.

December 16th.—The signallers got communication again with General Plumer and Colonel Pulteney to the north of Grootvlei. The usual fatigues. News of further captures by General Bruce Hamilton.

December 17th.—The usual fatigues. Signallers again in touch with General Plumer's Column, which had moved north-east in the direction of Spitz Kop.

December 18th.—The usual fatigues. Signallers again in touch with General Plumer. News received of further captures by General Bruce Hamilton north-east of Ermelo.

December 19th.—Usual fatigues. Signallers could not get communication with Columns north.

Lieut. Crossman was to have taken out a party to raid Boers at Waaiboek, but fog prevented him. Later information came that there were 70 Boers there.

December 20th.—Usual fatigues. Signallers could not get communication with Columns. News received from 14 Mounted Infantry that 2nd Lieut. L. P. Russell died of wounds received in action at Brakfontein on 19th inst.

The Commanding Officer notified that gifts had been sent out from Mayor and Mayoress of Bradford and Mrs. Fry.

December 21st.—Usual fatigues. The Commanding Officer notified that the Lady Mayoress of York was sending out gifts to the Battalion; also the receipt of £138 6s. 6d. from Officers, past and present of the Regiment, at home, through Colonel Noyes, Commanding 14th Regimental District.

December 22nd.—Sunday. No fatigues.

December 23rd.—The signallers got into communication with General Plumer, who signalled that he was driving south a force of about 500 to 600 Boers. All blockhouses were warned to be especially on the alert. In the afternoon the Boers could be clearly seen from Paarde Kop to be near Spitz Kop, with General Plumer's Force close behind; but owing to the fatigue of General Plumer's horses he could not push on.

December 24th.—Usual fatigues. No. 12a sangar fired last night at six Boers who tried to get from south to north. The Boers were driven back. There were no signs of the Boers from Paarde Kop. General Plumer appeared to be moving in the direction of Wakkerstroom. The following casualties, which occurred to the 14th Mounted Infantry at Brakfontein on 19th inst., were announced in Battalion Orders:—

KILLED.—No. 5224 Private J. Clapham, D Company.
DIED OF WOUNDS.—Lieut. L. P. Russell.

WOUNDED.

2nd Lieut. P. S. Fryer.

4958	Act. Corpl. R. H. Brough,	E	Company.
5626	Lce.-Corpl. Edwards,	H	,,
5205	Private Marshall,	D	,,
5182	Private W. Wood,	C	,,

MISSING.

5369	Private Keighley,	G	,,
5227	Private J. Pearce,	D	,,
4468	Private E. Miller,	D	,,

December 25th.—Christmas Day. There were no fatigues or work to-day. A thick fog, which prevented any signalling all day. Lord Kitchener wired to Commanding Officer to wish him and all Troops under his command " A very happy Christmas."

December 26th.—Major Cayley started this evening from " C " post (Amsterdam) with a small Force of the Regiment and 8th Hussars to destroy a Boer store of mealies. Usual fatigues.

December 27th.—Major Cayley returned to " C " post about noon, having destroyed 2 tons of mealies. Usual fatigues.

December 28th.—News received of a reverse to Colonel Firman's Column, near Harrismith, in a night attack by De Wet.
   Lieut. Welchman and Lieut. Warner, 8th Hussars, with the detachment 8th Hussars, went out at night to try and capture eight Boers.
   Captain P. E. Lowe left for a short leave of absence on medical certificate.

December 29th.—Sunday. Lieut. Welchman and his party returned about 10 a.m., having been unsuccessful. The Boers had evidently seen the black scout tracking them, so had left the farm at dusk, and gone in the direction of the Pongola Bosch. On the way back the Boers attempted to hold the party up, but they arrived back with no casualties. No fatigues.

December 30th.—Nothing of interest. Usual fatigues.

December 31st.—Rinderpest has broken out among the cattle of the Section. Privates Pearce and Miller are reported to have returned to Standerton unwounded. These are two of the men reported missing from the 14th Mounted Infantry after action of December 19th at Brakfontein.

1902.

January 1st.—Nothing to record. Usual fatigues.

January 2nd.—Signallers in communication with General Bruce Hamilton. Usual fatigues. Alarm guns were put up in various places on the wire fence.

January 3rd.—Signallers again in communication with General B. Hamilton and General Plumer. Usual fatigues.

January 4th.—Signallers in touch with General B. Hamilton, also with signallers of a Boer force near Boschbank. Usual fatigues.

January 5th.—Sunday Church Parade. Service in the morning, the Rev. Griffiths, Acting Chaplain, taking the Service.

January 6th.—Scouts having reported that 2 Boers were going to attempt to cross from north to south this evening, Lieut. Welchman went out, with a small patrol, to hold them up at a point he knew they would pass about four miles to the east of No. 18 blockhouse. Unfortunately, he arrived there too late, and saw the Boers just in front of him. He and Corporal Gibson followed them up, hoping to capture them against the wire fencing. However, a patrol from " B " post, under Lieut. Harrington, was waiting for the Boers near to No. 21 blockhouse. The Boers came quite close to the patrol and were called upon to surrender, but their horses wheeled round and they galloped off. The patrol opened fire, but they could not see in the dark whether they hit. The Boers, galloping back, passed Lieut. Welchman and Corporal Gibson, who also fired ; one Boer was believed to have been hit.

January 7th.—The usual fatigues during the day.

In the evening Captain Jennings, 8th Hussars, with 15 of his Men from "C" post, and Lieut. Warner, 8th Hussars, with 13 of his Men from Castrol Nek, met near No. 18 sangar, accompanied by Lieut. Welchman and native scouts. They went out to raid a farm—Goedgewonden—about 10 miles from the blockhouse line, where eight Boers were reported to be.

January 8th.—The 8th Hussars patrol arrived back near No. 18 blockhouse about noon, having captured one Boer, one rifle, two horses, about 70 rounds of small-arm ammunition, and about 200 sheep. The Boers were not at the farm, the scouts said, but at a farm only two miles this side of the Makattee's Kop. There they only found the one, but on the way back they searched the bush, and found signs of six Boers, who had just left, the fires being still burning. On the way back they were sniped by six Boers on outposts of Treuter's Commando, but there were no casualties. The patrol covered between 50 and 60 miles. Just the other side of Makattee's Kop was a Commando.

January 9th.—The usual fatigues. Nothing to record.

January 10th.—During the last two or three mornings two parties of Boers, each of about five men, have been seen by the scouts in or near a Kraal about 2,000 yards north of No. 9 blockhouse in the valley. A party of 24 Men, under Lieuts. Crossman and Bird, accompanied by Mr. De Jager, the intelligence agent, and native scouts, left the Nek at 8 p.m. to try and ambush these parties.

January 11th.—The party returned about 3 a.m., having discovered a very strong party of Boers. Having descended the cliff into the valley, and when within 800 yards of the Kraal, they noticed several small lights, as if pipes were being lit. The party was halted, and a scout sent on ahead. He returned with the information that there were about 300 Boers lying down within 800 yards of them. As this was considerably too large a force for the party to engage, they returned unnoticed by the Boers, owing to the thick fog.

January 12th.—No fatigues. A Boer boy, aged about 10, who came into "B" post, confirmed the information of about 300 burghers being in the vicinity of Waaihoek. He stated that he heard Commandant Opperman tell a burgher that they were going to attack Wakkerstroom one night from the south and west-south-west.

2nd Lieut. Smart returned to duty from Hospital.

January 13th.—The usual fatigues. 2nd Lieut. D. Grant-Dalton was sent into Hospital.

January 14th.—Usual fatigues. Nothing to record.

January 15th.—Usual fatigues.

January 16th.—Usual fatigues. Captain P. E. H. Lowe returned from leave to Durban.

January 17th.—Usual fatigues. Summary of news shows that the surrenders are increasing.

January 18th.—A thick fog. Nothing to record.

January 19th.—Sunday. No fatigues.

January 20th.—Lieut. Francis started with wagons for Volksrust. A Court of Investigation was held at Castrol Nek on the loss of B and E Companies' Pay Lists. During the night the wire fence was cut between Nos. W2 and W3 blockhouses.

January 21st.—Nothing to record.

January 22nd.—Ditto.

January 23rd.—Orders issued to collect as many Men of the Regiment here as possible for expedition to-morrow night.

January 24th.—During the course of the day Lieut. Boyall arrived with 20 Men from "B" post; Lieut. Welchman with 23 of B Company, and 22 of G Company, came. The sangars' garrisons were reduced to a minimum strength, all employed Men and the Men of "B" post being detailed for their garrison. Captain Jennings and Lieut. Howard, 8th Hussars, arrived with about 35 of their Men.

In the afternoon the Commanding Officer presented the Queen's pipe to the following:—

Sergt.-Major Roberts.	O.-R.-S. Hinchcliffe.
Cr.-Sergt. Kingsley.	Cr.-Sergt. Yates.
„ Ford.	„ Kerwin.
Sergt. Russell.	Sergt. Bartholomew.
„ Laracy.	„ Warwick.

The following are also to receive them:—

Arm.-Sergt. Southern.
Cr.-Sergt. Dawson.
„ Jackson.
Sergt. Naylor.
„ Read.
„ Leigh.

Sergt.-Dr. Teck.
Q.-M.-S. Jordan.
Cr.-Sergt. Valette.
Sergt. Casey.
„ Hunter.

January 24th.—At 9 p.m. Lieut.-Colonel Watts, with Lieuts. Crossman, Boyall, and Welchman, and about 80 N.C.O.'s and Men, left Camp to take up a position to the north of Castrol Nek and east of the Waaihoek Valley on Kroomhoek Ridge. Captain Jennings and the Hussars left at the same time to take up position in the Assegai Valley.

January 25th.—At 2 a.m. the Commanding Officer went out with 10 Men of the Battalion and 12-pounder B.L. Gun, under Captain Lambarde, Royal Garrison Artillery, to take up position under No. 7 blockhouse, whilst 20 Men of the Volunteers under Lieut. Huffam took up a position further along to the north-west on the same ridge. At the same time Lieut. Nicholson with 10 Men and signallers went up to Paarde Kop to establish a station to get into touch with Plumer's and Pulteney's Columns, working from the north, and Colville's from the east. All were in a position by 4 a.m. At dawn the Columns from the north surprised the Boers in the vicinity of Derdehoek and Waaihoek Farms. The Boers tried to break out to the east along the Assegai Valley, but were headed back by volleys from the 8th Hussars and the approach of the 26th Mounted Infantry from Colville's Column, and went back on to the northern end of Doornhoek, where they took cover under steep ground. They were shelled out of this by Plumer's Guns, and broke back along the ridge to the western and then to the south-western end of the ridge. On their way back they were shelled by Plumer's and Pulteney's Guns and Pom-poms, and also at extreme range by the 12-pounder near No. 7 blockhouse. Part of Plumer's Force then worked up from the Assegai Valley, coming down on the north-east of the Boers, while some of the Victorian Mounted Rifles of Pulteney's Column worked down from the Waaihoek Plateau to the west of them. 25 of the Boers then galloped across the deep valley that runs in a south-easterly direction from Waaihoek, and, approaching the Gun near No. 7 blockhouse, with a white flag, surrendered to the Commanding Officer. They were then marched to Castrol Nek. The 26th Mounted Infantry arrived later at Castrol Nek with 3 more prisoners, including Field Cornet Lens, of the Swaziland Commando, and Colonel Watts brought in Burgher Moolmann, who had been in correspondence about surrender for some time. Other small parties were captured by the Columns. The total captures amounted to 35 prisoners, with horses, rifles and ammunition, about 250 head of cattle, and a large number of sheep. All Men of the Regiment got back about noon, and, with the exception of the Men from "B" post, went back to their respective posts.

The following appeared in Battalion Orders:—

"The Commanding Officer wishes to thank all ranks for the energy and zeal they have shown last night and to-day in the operations which have ended so successfully."

January 26th.—Lieut. Boyall and the Men from "B" post returned to their stations. In the morning 26th Mounted Infantry left to rejoin Colville's Column. The prisoners were sent into Wakkerstroom, with the exception of Moolmann, who was allowed to go out again, as he said he could enable the Column to catch the Bothas.

January 27th.—The Columns would not trust Moolman, but he sent in to say that if he was allowed to stay out a little longer he would induce three or four others to surrender.

January 28th.—Moolman arrived back in the morning with three other burghers to surrender. Later in the day Corporal Riet van Oudtshoorn and another burgher arrived. 10 of the Swaziland Commando passed from south to north last night between Wakkerstroom and Wakkerstroom Nek. News received that General Viljoen has been captured.

January 29th.—In the afternoon about a dozen Boers were seen in the small bush to the north-east of Castrol Nek. Captain Jennings went out with a patrol of the 8th Hussars, but they left before he could reach them.

January 30th.—Nothing to record.

January 31st.—Ditto.

February 1st.—Ditto.

February 2nd.—Sunday. 15 Men from each of B, G, and K Companies came up in the day to relieve a corresponding number of H. At 2 p.m. Lieuts. Crossman, Welchman, and Bird, with 50 Men of H Company, started on an expedition to the farms round Waaihoek. Captain Jennings and about 35 Men, 8th Hussars, left at 3 p.m. for same purpose. They marched about seven miles in direction of Johnson's Hoek, and there halted till nightfall.

February 3rd.—About midnight the 8th Hussars and H Company raided the farms, Waaihoek, Derdehoek, and Vaalbank in succession, but found no burghers. The Boers were evidently not sleeping in the farms, but in a kloof, and had sufficient warning to escape. Two saddles were found and destroyed, as well as some clothing and blankets. On their way back the patrol was sniped at a long range, but there were no casualties. The Men of D, G, and K Companies returned to their posts in the afternoon.

Orders received to prepare a draft of 4 Sergeants, 6 Corporals, and 140 Men for the 1st Battalion in India, which will send us a like number in exchange.

February 4th and 5th.—Usual fatigue. Nothing to record.

February 6th.—An expedition, corresponding in numbers to that of February 2nd, was to have gone out to-night to Waaihoek, but, the native scouts not returning with information, it was postponed.

February 7th.—Usual fatigues. Nothing to record. Firing at night from No. 18 sangar, who said they heard men getting through the wire, which was not cut, however.

February 8th.—Usual fatigues. Official news received that part of Kekewich's Column have captured 131 of De la Rey's men, including Commandant Albert and Field Cornet Duplessis.

February 9th.—Collected 45 from H, G, and K Companies for garrison here. Captain Jennings, with his Men of 8th Hussars, and Lieuts. Crossman, Cuthell, Bird, and Smart, with 50 Men, left at 10 p.m. for expedition to Derdehoek and Vaalbank Farms.

February 10th.—The patrol returned in the afternoon, having been unsuccessful. Both the parties from here were in position by daybreak, and the Mounted Infantry from Wakkerstroom were on the ridge above Derdehoek, but on the latter opening fire the Boers slipped away to the north between the two parties. Fairly heavy fire at one time, but no casualties.

February 11th.—Official summary received that Boer losses last week amounted to 717; also description of operations against De Wet in Frankfort and Heilbron districts, which have resulted in the loss of 283 to De Wet.

February 12th.—Captain Ingpen with a draft of 40 Men arrived at Castrol from England. Captain Ingpen posted to G Company.

February 13th.—The Commanding Officer inspected the draft from England in the morning. Firing at Nos. 12, 13, and 14 blockhouses in the night. Six Boers from the Waaihoek Valley surrendered at Wakkerstroom.

February 14th.—The Men of the draft joined the Companies to which they had been posted.

The Boers, between this line and the Standerton-Ermelo line, are reported to have the intention of breaking south.

February 15th.—Brigadier-General Bullock arrived in the afternoon from Volksrust. Signallers were in communication with General Plumer, who is near Mooipoort.

February 16th.—Heavy firing (volley and independent) was heard from No. 12 blockhouse and No. 12 sangar from 3-35 a.m. to 4 a.m. The N.C.O.'s in charge of these two posts, Corporal Acton and Corporal Gray, reported, afterwards, that shortly after 3-30 a.m. the Alarm Gun on the trip wire across the road went off. On opening fire on the gate, fire was directed on No. 12 sangar from Boers near the drift over the Mabola, some 600 yards to the north-east of No. 12 sangar. The firing lasted for 20 minutes, and the Boers then withdrew to the north, having failed to get through. No casualties.

General Bullock left at 6 a.m. for Volksrust again, having been recalled. Captain Jennings and 2nd Lieut. Lindley and the detachment 8th Hussars left with him. The guide, De Jager, and native scouts found tracks of some 50 Boers at the drift through the Mabola.

February 17th.—Last night a party of Boers approached No. 18 sangar from the direction of Chance Farm. A break in the mist showed them to the sentry, who opened fire upon them. No. 18 sangar, No. 20 blockhouse, and No. 21 blockhouse all opened fire on the wire fence, and the Boers were driven back.

February 18th.—Summary of news received shows good captures and an increasing number of surrenders. Nothing to record. Usual fatigues.

February 19th.—Nothing to record.

February 20th.—At 7 a.m. 40 Men of the Battalion, under the command of the Commanding Officer, paraded and marched about six miles to the north, and took up position at Bloemhof. General Plumer was at Derdehoek, and Colonel Vialls, of his Column, was coming up the Assegai Valley from the east. Smoke from veldt fires completely obscured our view, and, at 1 p.m., hearing that Colonel Vialls had passed, the party returned to Castrol.

February 21st.—News received that General Plumer captured 12 Boers yesterday at Derdehoek, including Michael Harris and Theunis Botha. Usual fatigues.

February 22nd.—Nothing to record. Usual fatigues.

February 23rd.—Sunday. No fatigues.

February 24th.—Usual fatigues.

February 25th.—Ditto.

February 26th.—Early this morning firing was heard from No. 12 blockhouse and sangar. N.C.O.'s in charge reported, after day-break, that the Alarm Gun on east side of road gate went off; they opened fire on the road. At daybreak the wire fence and gate were found to be intact.

February 27th.—Nothing to record. Usual fatigues.

February 28th.—News received that operations against De Wet culminated yesterday in 819 Boers being killed and captured. Several Columns under General B. Hamilton arrived at Wakkerstroom.

March 1st.—Nothing to record. Usual fatigues.

March 2nd.—Sunday. No fatigues. Nothing to record.

March 3rd.—Captain Ingpen went to "C" post and took over command of D Company. Captain Lowe returned to Head Quarters and resumed command of B Company. Lieut. Cuthell took over command of G Company. G and B Companies exchanged blockhouses. B Company now has its Head Quarters at Castrol, and blockhouses on each side of the Nek. Boers attempted in the night to break from north to south between Nos. 33 and 34 blockhouses; about six succeeded.

March 4th.—Summary of news received to-day gives the largest number of surrenders, prisoners, &c., for a week since the capture of Prinsloo's Force—just on 1,100. Nothing to record. Usual fatigues.

March 5th.—Firing in the night from No. 12 sangar. Report in the morning it was only at stray cattle. Nothing to record. Big Guns heard to the south-east.

Gifts for the Regiment have been received from the Lady Mayoress of Bradford and Mrs. Slade.

March 6th.—Very heavy firing from 9-15 to 10-30 p.m. last night from Nos. 13 and 14 blockhouses and No. 14 sangar. Report in the morning that three Boers sniped the sentry at No. 14 blockhouse from the north, and that when the blockhouses opened fire the enemy from the south also commenced. Bullet marks on the south side of the wall of the sangar show that the Boers did fire from the south. No casualties, and wire not cut. 18 Men, who had been serving with the 4th Battalion, joined the Battalion.

March 7th.—The Men who joined yesterday were sent out to "C" post to relieve as many Men as possible of the Indian draft at the farthest end of the line.

March 8th.—Firing at many parts of the line last night. About 9 p.m. Lieut. Cuthell reported heavy firing from No. 18 sangar and No. 20 blockhouse. It only lasted about ten minutes. A few minutes afterwards a few shots were fired from No. 12 sangar, and a little later on No. 5 blockhouse reported firing from direction of No. 3. From reports in the day it appears that the firing was mostly at stray cattle.

March 9th.—Sunday. No fatigues. Nothing to record.

March 10th.—Heavy firing at No. 18 sangar and blockhouses near. Spoor of Boers, but no crossing was effected. The Alarm Guns went off, and they fired on to the spot, preventing any Boers from crossing.

No. 18 sangar was heavily fired at, and fired a rocket at the place where Boers were thought to be, and Nos. 20 and 21 took up the firing on seeing the rocket. Usual fatigues.

March 11th.—Usual fatigues. The draft for India began to be collected at Castrol Nek.

March 12th.—Draft from India expected to arrive at Durban to-morrow.

March 13th.—Indian draft all collected at Castrol Nek, and adjoining blockhouses.

March 14th.—Nothing to record. Usual fatigues. Lieut.-Colonel Bethell, Inspector-General of Blockhouses, arrived at Castrol Nek on tour of inspection.

March 15th.—Nothing to record. Usual fatigues.

March 16th.—Sunday. Usual fatigues. The Commanding Officer inspected the kits and equipment of Men of draft for India. Lieut. A. H. Cuthell, returning to No. 15 blockhouse from Castrol Nek at dusk, was wounded by Alarm Gun at gate near No. 12 blockhouse, the bullet entering near his hips.

March 17th.—Nothing to record.

March 18th.—Captain Paget and 146 N.C.O.'s and Men arrived at Castrol Nek from India about noon. The draft was inspected by the Commanding Officer on arrival in the afternoon. Men of the incoming draft were sent down to Nos. 6, 8, 8a, and 12 blockhouses, to relieve Men of the outgoing draft. Captain Paget was posted to G Company.

March 19th.—Lieut. G. L. Crossman left with 150 N.C.O.'s and Men of the draft for India. Lieut. Crossman was to take them to Durban and there hand them over to an Officer on board the ss. "Syria." The draft was inspected and addressed by the Commanding Officer, who, in bidding them "Good-bye," thanked them for their good conduct in field and garrison, and for their gallantry in action during the course of their Campaign of nearly two and a-half years.

Appointment of Lieut. H. O. L. Nicholson, D.S.O., as Adjutant, vice Captain A. C. Daly, dated 1st August, 1901.

March 20th.—Usual fatigues. Nothing to record. Captain J. B. Paget went to No. 15 blockhouse, and assumed command of D Company.

March 21st.—Lieut. Crossman and draft left Volksrust this morning. Usual fatigues.

March 22nd.—Draft was distributed between the Companies.

March 23rd.—Sunday, no fatigues. Nothing to record. A few Boers tried on the night of the 22nd to cross from north to south between No. 32 blockhouse and "C" post, but were driven back.

March 24th.—Usual fatigues. Nothing to record.

March 25th.—Ditto.

March 26th.—Ditto.

March 27th.—Usual fatigues. News received that Schalk Burger, Kreoge, Lucas Meyer, and Reitz have gone to Pretoria.

March 28th.—Nothing to record. Usual fatigues.

March 29th.—Firing during the night from No. 18 sangar and No. 21 blockhouse. Sentry at the former heard the sounds of moving horses, and the Alarm Gun at drift, 300 yards away, went off. Sangar and blockhouse immediately fired along the wire. In the morning the wire was found to be correct. Blockhouse further along the line towards "B" post also took up the firing.

Lieut. G. L. Crossman returned from Durban, having handed the draft over on board the ss. "Syria."

March 30th.—Sunday. No fatigues. News that the Boer Government have left Pretoria for Kroonstadt to see Steyn.

March 31st.—Usual fatigues. Nothing to record. Took over Nos. 33 and 34 blockhouses from the 2nd Scots Guards.

April 1st.—Usual fatigues. A party of about 80 Boers being reported a few miles from No. 15 blockhouse, it was thought probable that they might attempt to cross near No. 18 sangar, and a party of one N.C.O. and 10 Men were sent to drift near No. 18. No attempt was made, however.

April 2nd.—Usual fatigues. Frequent firing in the early part of the night from Nos. 18, 20, 16, and 14 blockhouses. Report in the morning from Captain Paget, No. 15 blockhouse, as follows :—

No. 20 blockhouse reported horseman seen on Helpmakaar Road, about 6-30 p.m. No. 18 blockhouse reported they were sniped from the east corner of their position at about 6-30 p.m. No. 18 sangar was also sniped from same position. No. 18 sangar reported seeing two mounted men north at about 6-15 p.m. No. 16 blockhouse was apparently sniped by these two men. The fence at No. 14 blockhouse was touched, which thereupon opened fire; fire was returned from south.

No. 14 sangar was fired at about 7 p.m. They saw Boers to the south of them. Sniping continued at intervals until about 10 p.m. Nos. 16 and 17 blockhouses saw nothing, but on hearing fire, fired down the wire. The only wire that was cut was at No. 14 sangar, and apparently that by our bullets.

The Commanding Officer went down to " C " post on tour of inspection.

April 3rd.—The Commanding Officer returned in the afternoon. Boers were reported in the valley below No. 15 blockhouse. This morning a little firing reported during the night round No. 18 sangar.

April 4th.—Usual fatigues. Nothing to record.

April 5th.—Lieuts. Crossman, Bird, and Smart, with 15 mounted and 25 dismounted Men, collected at No. 15 blockhouse. Scouts, however, reported that Boers had departed, so the Men returned to their post. Later there was firing from No. 18 sangar, but no Boers got through.

April 6th.—F Company took over No. 34 blockhouse from the Scots Guards and built a new sangar there.

April 7th.—Nothing to record. Usual fatigues.

April 8th.—Ditto.

April 9th.—New blockhouse was built between Nos. 35 and 34, and garrisoned by F Company. No. 35 blockhouse taken over from Scots Guards.

April 10th.—Nothing to record.

April 11th.—The Commanding Officer presented, on parade, medals for distinguished conduct in the field to Cr.-Sergts. Kingsley and Ford.

April 12th.—Colonel Colville's Column encamped for the night near No. 15 blockhouse.

April 13th.—Sunday. No fatigues. Lieut.-Colonel Fry left for Durban on 30 days' leave. Colonel Colville's Column passed through in the morning on its way to Wakkerstroom.

April 14th.—Usual fatigues. Nothing to record.

April 15th.—General Bullock and A.D.C. arrived from Volksrust on tour of inspection, and stayed at Castrol Nek for the night.

April 16th.—General Bullock went on this morning to "C" post. New blockhouse built between No. 18 sangar and No 21 blockhouse.

April 17th.—No. 16 blockhouse dismantled. Usual fatigues. Nothing to record.

April 18th.—Surprise sangar built between No. 20a (new blockhouse) and No. 21, only to be used in case of expected crossing. 22 Volunteers under Lieut. Hill arrived from England.

April 19th.—Nothing to record.

April 20th.—Ditto.

April 21st.—Captain W. A. Pearson (Volunteer Service Company), having received permission to return home, left this morning. Lieut. Huffam took over the command of the Company. General Bullock arrived back. News received that Boer delegates have gone out again to the Commandos, and orders received to allow armed Boers, with flag of truce, having pass signed by Commandant-General Louis Botha and stamped with Lord Kitchener's office stamp, through the line. It is understood that Boers are holding meetings to consider the terms offered. Feeling is hopeful.

April 22nd.—Nothing to record. Usual fatigues.

April 23rd.—Ditto.

April 24th.—Ditto.

April 25th.—Ditto.

April 26th.—Mr. Pretorius, Intelligence Agent, left "B" post to ride back here. He had not returned by dusk, and "B" post sent up message to say that his horse had been found on the further side of Assegai River.

April 27th.—Lieut. Stade found Mr. Pretorius at foot of No. 25 hill this morning. He was unconscious, and remained so all day.

April 28th.—Nothing to record. Guide Pretorius brought up here, and sent into Wakkerstroom, still unconscious.

April 29th.—Captain Ingpen met General Louis Botha passing through blockhouse line near No. 36, and handed to him a telegram from Lord Kitchener relating to matters concerning the conference to be held at Vereeniging on May 15th.

April 30th.—Nothing to record. Usual fatigues. Cable information received that Major J. C. Yale has been posted to the command of 1st Battalion, and Brevet Lieut.-Colonel Watts second in command of the 2nd Battalion.

May 1st.—Major Yale left for Maritzburg on leave, and Lieut.-Colonel Watts took over temporary command of the Battalion.

May 2nd.—Nothing to record. Usual fatigues.

May 3rd.—Sunday. No fatigues.

May 4th.—Nothing to record. Usual fatigues.

May 5th.—Ditto.

May 6th.—Ditto.

May 7th.—Ditto.

May 8th.—Lieut. Francis left for Volksrust for 10 days' leave.

May 9th.—Nothing to record. Usual fatigues.

May 10th.—Ditto.

May 11th.—Sunday. No fatigues.

May 12th.—Nothing to record. Usual fatigues.

May 13th.—The Commanding Officer returned from leave. The usual fatigues.

May 14th.—Nothing to record. Usual fatigues.

May 15th.—Draft of 69 N.C.O.'s and Men arrived from England. Lieuts. Crossman and Smart, with 15 mounted Men, made a night raid on Derdehoek Farm, and captured one Boer, one rifle, some small-arm ammunition, one saddle, and three horses.

May 16th.—Draft distributed between the Companies. B Company took over the blockhouses extending from Castrol Nek to No. 19 blockhouse ; G Company, blockhouses from No. 18 sangar to " B" post.

May 17th.—E Company took over blockhouses hitherto occupied by A Company. The latter Company marched to Castrol Nek. Lieut. Smart left for Heidelburg to join 14th Mounted Infantry, relieving Lieut. E. F. Grant-Dalton.

May 18th.—A Company took over the blockhouses occupied by the 2nd Volunteer Service Company. In the afternoon the Volunteers collected at Wakkerstroom. Lieut. Cuthell rode out in the morning under a flag of truce to find Vryheid or Utrecht Commandos. He found a patrol of about 30 men near Makatees Kop, under V. C. Nortje, and handed them letters for both Commandos, notifying them that, under instructions from Lord Kitchener, the two Commandos are immune from attack till further orders, and that British Commanders have orders to keep the natives of the district in order as much as possible. Lieut. Cuthell stayed the night with the Boers and returned next day.

May 19th.—The Volunteers proceeded to Volksrust, *en route* for England. Usual fatigues.

May 20th and 21st.—Nothing to record. Usual fatigues.

May 22nd.—Lieut. and Adjutant O. H. L. Nicholson left on 15 days' leave to Durban. Usual fatigues.

May 23rd.—Nothing to record. Usual fatigues.

May 24th.—Commanding Officer left for Volksrust on two days' leave. Lieut.-Colonel Watts proceeded to Volksrust to take over command of that place. Usual fatigues.

May 25th.—Nothing to record. Sunday. No fatigues.

May 26th.—Commanding Officer returned from Volksrust. Lieut. E. F. Grant-Dalton returned from 14th Mounted Infantry. Usual fatigues.

May 27th.—Lieut. Francis returned from Volksrust from leave, bringing out Regimental Transport. Usual fatigues. Mail arrived with parcel of books and papers from T.R.H. Prince and Princess of Wales.

May 28th.—Nothing to record. Usual fatigues.

May 29th.—Captain P. E. H. Lowe proceeded to Wakkerstroom as Member of a Court of Inquiry assembled there. 2nd Lieut. E. T. Welchman returned to Battalion from sick leave. Usual fatigues.

May 30th.—Nothing to record. Usual fatigues.

May 31st.—Captain P. E. H. Lowe returned from Wakkerstroom. Usual fatigues.

June 1st.—News received that peace had been signed previous night. Great difficulty in sending messages to " B " and "C" posts, a terrific hurricane blowing; telegraph office blown away; nearly every tent in Camp destroyed.

June 2nd.—Orders arrived to send one Officer (Lieut.-Colonel Watts) and three N.C.O.'s (Sergeants Warwick and Lintott and Corporal Walker) and seven Privates (O'Neill, Berry, Foster, Addy, Briggs, Gowland, and Helstrop) home to represent Regiment at the Coronation. The detachment sail from Capetown on ss. " Bavarian."

June 3rd.—Coronation party left this morning, leaving Volksrust at 5 p.m. to-day. Message received through Lord Kitchener from the King, thanking all Troops for their efforts in bringing the war to so glorious and successful an issue.

June 4th.—2nd Lieut. Best joined, and was posted to E Company.

June 5th.—Orders received to have a Company concentrated ready to proceed to Volksrust. B Company collected at the Nek. No. 20a blockhouse, No. 18 sangar, and No. 19 blockhouse were vacated. G Company took over Nos. 18, 17, and 15 blockhouses. H Company took over Nos. 12, 13, and 14 blockhouses. Nos. 12, 14, and 15 sangars withdrawn. A Company vacated No. 1a and No. 8 blockhouse. No. 4a sangar vacated, and Garrison distributed over A Company's line.

June 6th.—Lieut. and Adjutant O. H. L. Nicholson returned to duty from leave.

The following Order by Lieut.-Colonel Fry, C.B., Commanding Battalion, was published on June 2nd, 1902 :—

"Notification having been received that peace has been signed, I take this opportunity of thanking the Officers, N.C.O.'s, and Men of the Battalion for their splendid conduct throughout this long and trying Campaign, both in action, on

4

the march, and during the trying and monotonous work on the blockhouse line. Officers and Men have throughout shown a true soldierly spirit, and have not only maintained the good name of the old Regiment, but have very largely added to it. There is no Regiment in South Africa that bears a better name for hard fighting, hard work, and good discipline than the West Yorkshire Regiment. This is not only my own opinion, but I have heard the same from the various Generals under whom we have served, including Lord Kitchener and General Lyttelton, and from many sources in England. I feel sure that all ranks agree with me in feeling a deep sense of pride in having belonged to the West Yorkshire Regiment. I hope and trust that in a very short time the Regiment will return to England. I feel confident that all Yorkshiremen will find, as they deserve, that their country fully appreciates all that they have done for their country. I hope that during the short time we may yet be in this country that all ranks will join in keeping up the fine state of discipline and cheerful obedience to orders that has been a marked characteristic of the Regiment throughout the Campaign. Let us all strive to make the name of the Regiment as good in peace as it has been in war.

"I wish every Officer and Man of the Regiment, which I have had the great honour to command, the best of luck and a speedy return to England."

June 7th.—The wire fences between blockhouses having to be removed, a start was made to-day.

B Company, under Captain Lowe, and band and drums left for Volksrust.

June 8th.—Nothing to record.

June 9th.—The following congratulatory message to Lord Kitchener and his Army was published in Orders :—

"His Majesty's Government offer to you their most sincere congratulations on the energy, skill, and patience with which you have conducted this prolonged Campaign, and would wish you to communicate to the Troops under your orders their profound sense of the spirit of endurance with which they have met every call upon them, of their bravery in action, of the excellent discipline preserved, and of the humanity shown by them throughout this trying period."

June 10th.—Nothing to record. Fatigues on dismantling wire fence.

June 11th.—Very rapid progress has been made in dismantling the fence.

Commandant Swart arrived at Castrol to arrange about bringing his Commando in.

June 12th.—General surrender of Wakkerstroom and Standerton Boers took place at Naude Farm to-day. General B. Hamilton received the surrender. Commandant Louis Botha was present.

June 13th.—The following telegram from H.R.H. The Prince of Wales to Lord Kitchener, and the latter's reply, were published in Orders :—

"Most heartily do I congratulate you and your Army on satisfactory termination of hostilities."

"I beg to thank your Royal Highness for your kind message, which will be most appreciated by the Army."

June 14th.—Nothing to record.

June 15th.—2nd Lieut. A. W. Lupton promoted Lieut., vice J. E. Gretton seconded (*London Gazette*, 26th April, 1902).

The following farewell order was published in Orders:—

"On relinquishing command of Natal, General Lyttelton wishes to place on record his warm appreciation of the good work done by all ranks serving under him since he assumed command nine months ago. His thanks are specially due to the Officers commanding Sub-Districts, the Heads of Departments, the Head Quarters, and their Staff. The duties they have carried out have been important and arduous, and the immunity of Natal from serious attacks has been much due to the excellence of the arrangements made to repel any attempts at invasion, though, with exceptions, the Troops have not been actively engaged, they have had much hard and irksome work to do. They have done it well, and their behaviour in quarters has been very good. All have contributed to making General Lyttelton's term of command pleasant to him, and he gives it up with regret."

June 16th.—Major and Brevet Lieut.-Colonel H. E. Watts has been appointed second in command of the 2nd Battalion West Yorkshire Regiment, vice Major J. E. Yale, D.S.O., promoted.

June 17th.—Nothing to record.

June 18th.—Lieut. A. M. Boyall left to supervise the erection of headstones to Officers and Men who fell in Natal.

June 19th.—Nothing to record.

June 20th.—Lieut.-Colonel Fry, C.B., proceeded to Volksrust on duty as President of a Military Court. Major Cayley came to Castrol to take command.

June 21st.—Nothing to record.

June 22nd.—Notification received that surrender of burghers in Orange River Colony and Transvaal were now complete.

June 23rd.—Nothing to record.

June 24th.—In the evening orders were received to send off at once the first 100 Reservists on the Roll, compiled according to instruction received *re* demobilization; this first batch includes all Men belonging to Section D.

June 25th.—Notification received that H.M. The King being seriously ill, the Coronation is postponed.

June 26th.—Lord Kitchener issued a farewell order to the Army in South Africa on June 23rd. The order was received by us to-day. Lieut. G. L. Crossman and the first batch of 100 Reservists left Castrol for Volksrust.

June 27th.—Nothing to record.

June 28th.—Head Quarters, A and E Companies, and all Reservists left Castrol Nek for Volksrust. Captain Paget was in command of this party. Halted for the night at Wakkerstroom.

June 29th.—Head Quarters, A and G Companies, and Reservists arrived at Volksrust.

June 30th.—Captain A. C. Daly and Lieut. G. L. Crossman left by train with 100 Reservists for Durban, *en route* for England. Captain Spry rejoined the Battalion from the Staff.

July 1st.—Nil.

July 2nd.—H Company arrived at Volksrust from Castrol Nek. " C " post is now clear of wire, stores, &c.

> The Battalion, for the present, is distributed as follows:—
> A, G, and H Companies and Reservists at Volksrust.
> B Company at Laing's Nek.
> F and E Companies at Castrol Nek.
> C and D Companies at " B " post.

July 3rd.—The following extract from a letter from General Bullock to the Commanding Officer was published in Battalion Orders:—

> " I wish you to express to all your Officers, N.C.O.'s, and Men my great appreciation of the very good work they have done in the Sub-District, both during the construction and occupation of the blockhouse line."

July 4th.—Nil.

July 5th.—Major E. Layton, with D, E, and C Companies, took over the Garrison of Wakkerstroom, " B " post being clear. B Company, under Captain Lowe, rejoined Head Quarters at Volksrust from Laing's Nek.

July 6th.—Nil.

July 7th.—Nil.

July 8th.—Intimation received from War Office that Sergeant-Major W. A. Roberts is promoted Quarter-Master with the honorary rank of Lieutenant, with effect from 1st May, 1902.

July 9th.—Lieut. E. F. Grant-Dalton was appointed Acting Adjutant and Quarter-Master of the Detachment at Wakkerstroom.

July 10th.—Nothing to record.

July 11th.—Ditto.

July 12th.—Ditto.

July 13th.—Sunday. Church Parade.

July 14th.—Companies exercised during the week in Physical Drill, Squad Drill, and Rifle Exercise.

July 15th.—Nothing to record.

July 16th.—Ditto.

July 17th.—Ditto.

July 18th.—Leave of absence to England on private affairs granted to the following Officers for four months from date of leaving Station :—

> Captain Spry, D.S.O.
>   „   P. E. H. Lowe.
> Lieut. G. L. Crossman.
>   „   A. M. Boyall, D.S.O.
>   „   J. G. Lemon.
>   „   A. W. Lupton.
> 2nd Lieut. A. H. G. Bird.

The second batch of Reservists—100 N.C.O.'s and Men, under Lieut. Crossman and Lieut. Cuthell (who is to join the 14th Regimental Depôt)—left Volksrust for Maritzburg, *en route* for England.

Lieut. A. M. Ross rejoined the Battalion from the Brigade Depôt at Pietermaritzburg.

July 19th.—Nothing to record.

July 20th.—Sunday. Church Parade.

July 21st.—Companies exercised ensuing week in Skirmishing Drill and Firing Exercise.

July 22nd.—Nothing to record.

July 23rd.—Ditto.

July 24th.—Nil.

July 25th.—The Detachment from Castrol Nek and Wakkerstroom, being relieved by the 33rd Battalion Imperial Yeomanry. rejoined the Battalion at Volksrust to-day.

July 26th.—Nothing to record.

July 27th.—Sunday Church Parade.

July 28th.—Nothing to record.

July 29th.—Ditto.

July 30th.—Orders received for the Battalion to proceed by march route to Newcastle.

August 1st.—2nd Lieut. Bird with advanced party proceeded by rail to-day to Newcastle.

Lieut.-Colonel W. Fry, C.B., granted 10 days' leave on Medical Certificate.

Major Cayley assumes command of Battalion.

August 2nd.—Reveille sounded at 4-30 a.m. Camp was struck immediately afterwards, and the Battalion paraded at 5-45 a.m. for the march to Newcastle. The Quarter-Master, with cooks and pioneers, marched on ahead, and breakfasts were ready at Laing's Nek for the Battalion. The Battalion arrived at Mount Prospect about 12 noon and encamped.

August 3rd.—Reveille sounded at 4-30 a.m. Camp was struck immediately afterwards.

The Battalion marched at 5-30 a.m. Breakfasts were served on the road near Ingogo stream. The Battalion arrived at Botha's Pass about 11 a.m. and encamped.

August 4th.—Reveille sounded at 4-30 a.m. Camp was struck immediately afterwards. The Battalion marched at 5-30 a.m. Breakfasts were served on the road. The Battalion arrived at Newcastle about 11 a.m., and Camp was pitched at Kitchener's Kopje, about one and a-half miles to the north-west of the town.

TOTAL CASUALTIES OF THE 2ND BATTALION THE PRINCE OF WALES'S OWN (WEST YORKSHIRE REGIMENT)

During the South African War, October 20th, 1899, to June 1st, 1902.

1.—KILLED IN ACTION.

Officers .. .. 4 }
Non-Commissioned Officers and Men .. 67 } Total, 71

2.—DIED OF WOUNDS.

Officer .. .. 1 }
Non-Commissioned Officers and Men .. 10 } Total, 11

3.—DIED OF DISEASE.

Officers .. .. nil }
Non-Commissioned Officers and Men .. 57 } Total, 57

Total deaths 139

4.—WOUNDED.

Officers .. .. 16 }
Non-Commissioned Officers and Men .. 250 } Total, 266

5.—VOLUNTEER SERVICE COMPANY (ATTACHED).

Died of disease .. .. 3 } Total,
Accidentally wounded .. 2 } 3 deaths, 2 wounded.

2ND WEST YORKSHIRE REGIMENT.

KILLED IN ACTION.

OFFICERS (4).

RANK.	NAMES.	PLACE.	DATE.
Captain	C. Ryall	Rangeworthy	21/1/00
,,	T. Berney	Monte Christo	18/2/00
Major	H. T. De C. Hobbs ..	Honing Spruit	22/6/00
Lieut.	M. G. Cantor	Bothwell	6/2/01

DIED OF WOUNDS.

OFFICER (1).

2nd Lieut.	L. P. Russell	Holland	19/12/01

KILLED IN ACTION.

NON-COMMISSIONED OFFICERS AND MEN (67).

REGTL. No.	RANK AND NAME.	PLACE.	DATE.
5198	Lce.-Corpl. H. Whiteley ..		
5136	Pte. J. Benson		
2966	Dr. H. Russell		
2294	Pte. J. W. Newton	Willow Grange ..	23/11/99
5129	,, J. Thornton		
2435	,, J. Smith		
2250	,, W. Morgan		
5416	,, T. Tobin		
5010	,, F. Crosier		
5364	,, W. Gascoigne		
2679	,, E. Kershaw	Rangeworthy	21/1/00
3403	,, F. Owen		
3917	,, W. Buckle		
5504	,, W. Hague	Cingolo	17/2 00
4782	Lce.-Corpl. J. Mathers		
3199	Pte. J. Howitt		
5022	,, J. Vaughan	Monte Christo ..	18/2/00
1144	,, W. Brass		
4726	Corpl. J. H. Silcock		

KILLED IN ACTION—Continued.

REGTL. No.	RANK AND NAME.	PLACE.	DATE.
3544	Pte. F. Freele ..		
2105	,, C. Fallon ..	Pieter's Hill ..	27/2/00
1750	Sergt. F. Poplar		
5471	Pte. J. Loftus ..	Sundays River	10/4/00
5403	,, M. Flanaghan ..	Botha's Pass ..	8/6/00
2430	Corpl. G. Anderson		
5300	Lce.-Corpl. F. Turner ..		
3254	Pte. G. Thornton		
1032	,, M. Ward ..		
5054	Lce. Corpl. T. Dodd ..		
3916	Pte. A. Russell ..	Buffel's Poort..	3/12/00
2594	,, W. Heaphy		
4495	Sergt. A. Mountain		
5230	Corpl. T. Hey ..		
2884	Pte. M. Langan		
2322	Corpl. H. Taylor		
3228	,, R. Martlew		
5387	Pte. W. Stead ..		
5002	,, S. Lindley		
5526	,, J. Myers ..		
4512	,, H. Dyson ..		
5333	,, W. Fletcher		
5064	,, A. Middleton		
5994	,, H. Onslow ..		
2101	Sergt. G. Greensmith ..	Bothwell	6/2/01
5676	Corpl. E. Deglow		
3165	Pte. B. Knight ..		
951	,, M. Hurton		
4464	,, A. Sear ..		
5899	,, H. Stokes ..		
5901	,, H. Hawksby		
5673	,, J. Crosby ..		
2518	,, J. Snead ..		
4373	,, H. Clarkson		
5239	,, W. Brown ..		7/2/01
4617	,, W. Smith ..		10/4/01
5577	Lce.-Corpl. S. Weston..		
2961	Pte. R. Atkinson		
2850	,, J. Anderson		
2630	,, M. Curley ..		
5056	,, W. Hope ..	Railway Accident, Pretoria ..	7/6/01
5815	,, G. Rodwell		
1738	,, G. Redmond		
3098	,, J. Jackson		
5851	,, A. Acroyd ..		
5120	,, A. Foster ..		6/7/01
5224	,, J. Clapham	Holland	19/12/01
5090	,, J. Banks ..	Lindley	8/5/02

DIED OF WOUNDS.

NON-COMMISSIONED OFFICERS AND MEN (9).

Regtl. No.	Rank and Name.	Place.	Date.
2616	Pte. A. Dixon	Willow Grange	23/11/99
2587	,, A. Rudd	,, ,, ...	,,
2360	Corpl. M. Barwell	,, ,, ...	,,
3099	Pte. W. Gibbs	Estcourt	26/11/99
2920	,, H. Page	York	21/12/01
5149	,, A. Smith		29/2/00
4855	Lce.-Corpl. M. Till	Mooi River	9/5/00
4946	Pte. W. Hayes	Ermelo	26/2/00
2928	,, T. Marshall	Newcastle	2/7/01

DIED OF DISEASE.

OFFICERS (Nil).

MEN (57).

Regtl. No.	Rank and Name.	Place.	Date.
1788	Pte. W. A. Smith	Machadodorp	27/3/01
2935	,, S. Beresford	Mooi River	21/2/00
5229	,, W. Smith	At Sea	15/9/01
4666	,, W. Greenwood	Pretoria	7/12/01
2551	,, G. Thornton	Charlestown ..	13/12/01
5194	Lce.-Corpl. L. Cupitt .. .	Pietermaritzburg ..	24/1/00
3585	Pte. G. M. Kelly	Newcastle	26/5/00
2999	,, J. Hall	Mooi River	27/5/00
4430	,, T. Brown	Standerton	20/6/00
1993	Lce.-Sergt. W. J. Hammond..	ss. " Roslin Castle " ..	31/11/99
5602	Pte. J. Merry	Charlestown	11/3/02
1742	,, L. Booth	,, ...	4/2/02
4666	,, W. McGuire	Wakkerstroom	14/2/02
3139	,, J. W. Prest	ss. " Simla "	12/5/00
5185	,, J. Wood	Ladysmith	27/3/00
1393	,, R. Hemsley	Chieveley..	11/4/00
4826	,, C. H. Ryder	ss. " Lismore Castle " ..	16/4/00
5664	,, J. Dawson..	Chieveley..	9/5/00
1041	,, T. Cooper	Middleburg	6/5/01
5924	,, W. Killarney	,, ...	3/5/01
3861	,, A. Stevenson	Volksrust..	19/7/02
5742	,, J. Cotter	Castrol Nek	5/7/02
2955	,, W. Tigell	Charlestown	30/4/02
3575	,, E. Kelly	Dundee	26/5/00
2543	,, J. Dockray	Middleburg	24/9/00
4777	,, T. Taylor	Rustenburg	12/10/00
5326	,, H. Schulze	,, ...	26/10/00
2415	,, G. Heeley	,, ...	22/11/00
5874	., F. Stephenson	Pretoria	26/5/01
5116	Lce.-Corpl. W. Fryer	,, ...	18/6/01

DIED OF DISEASE—Continued

REGTL. No.	RANK AND NAME.	PLACE.	DATE.
2075	Pte. T. Callaghan	Mooi River	10/8 00
5916	„ H. Skilliter	Rietfontein	5/1 01
5220	Corpl. F. Mostyn	Pretoria ..	12/10/01
4551	„ J. Gilling	Rustenburg	1/1/01
5249	Lce.-Corpl. C. H. Montressor..	Pretoria ..	23 1/01
5552	Pte. H. Marsh ..	Rustenburg	27/1/01
4466	„ G. Deverson	Middleburg	30/1/01
5740	„ W. Whitehead	Bloemfontein	18/2/01
5847	„ C. Copley ..	Middleburg	19/2/01
5746	„ F. Rolfe ..	Bloemfontein	20/2/01
5544	„ J. Roberts..	Pretoria ..	5 1 01
1644	„ J. Chadwick	Middleburg	27/2 01
5703	„ R. Hamilton	Standerton	2,3/01
150	„ W. Hall ..	At Sea ..	11/1 00
5310	„ E. Bradbury	Ladysmith	6/5/00
5386	„ J. Scott ..	„	27/4/00
4616	„ W. Wiffin ..	At Sea ..	9/11/99
1681	Lce.-Corpl. W. Walker	Middleburg	9/1/01
4874	Pte. W. Chapman	Pretoria ..	7/2 01
2908	„ J. Crowther	Standerton	4/3 01
5907	„ J. Huthinson	Wakkerstrcom	13/4/01
5948	„ R. White ..	Newcastle	12/4/01
5255	„ J. Hammond	Middleburg	4/5/01
2431	„ W. Wilson..	Johannesburg	30/7/01
5707	„ A. Harrison	Wakkerstroom	27/2/02
3626	„ R. Houston		13/10/01
5091	„ G. D. Bell..		3/6/01

WOUNDED.

Officers	.. ..	..	16
Non-Commissioned Officers and Men ..		..	250
	TOTAL ..	..	266

Printed by the Yorkshire Herald Newspaper Company, Limited,
9, Coney Street, York.